United States History Atlas

HAMMOND®
INCORPORATED
MAPLEWOOD, NEW JERSEY   07040

Introduction

The *United States History Atlas* was developed to help the student discover the geographic patterns underlying much of our nation's history. Using the maps and diagrams of this atlas, the student will develop a feeling of involvement in the great territorial, geopolitical and economic questions that constitute the American story. Such involvement should motivate the student to inquire on his own, into the geographic factors that underlie 400 years of political, economic and social life on this continent.

It will be noted that the contents of this atlas consist of far more than simple political maps merely showing political boundaries and towns at various dates. Instead, the maps and diagrams bring out the economic, social, demographic and ecological factors that have molded American history. For example, the maps of *Colonial America in 1770* on pages 12 and 13 present not only the boundaries of the thirteen colonies but, also, cartographic representation of colonial settlement patterns at three different dates, distribution maps showing the colonial economy, and an ethnic map illustrating the cultural diversity of the Atlantic seaboard area in the eighteenth century. Many other maps and graphs in the atlas bring out the socio-geographic elements of various periods in our history.

The sequence of maps in the atlas is broadly chronological, beginning with maps portraying the major Indian tribes and families and ending with maps and diagrams depicting current urban problems, economic data and election results. However, many topical maps, covering long periods of time, appear throughout the work. Thus the map of *Expansion of the United States* on page 16 shows the territorial growth of our nation from 1783 to 1898 — a single topic through 116 years of time. The maps entitled *Growth of Industry and Cities* on pages 34 and 35 cover modern industrial and urban development from its beginning at the time of the Civil War to the present decade. At the end of the atlas is a useful index locating specific place names important in American history.

The publishers of this wholly new teaching tool have succeeded in producing maps and graphs that are notable for their conciseness, legibility and scholarship. The type faces used for place names on the maps are distinguished for their clarity and large size. Colors have been selected to delineate clearly one geographic area from another. Confusing detail and overcrowding have been avoided by creating several maps for each topic and period of American history. Many of the maps indicate terrain by a shaded relief technique, so that the student will be made aware of the influence of topography on the events and movements of history. The result is a historical atlas that is both eye-pleasing and authoritative.

Contents

Introduction U-2

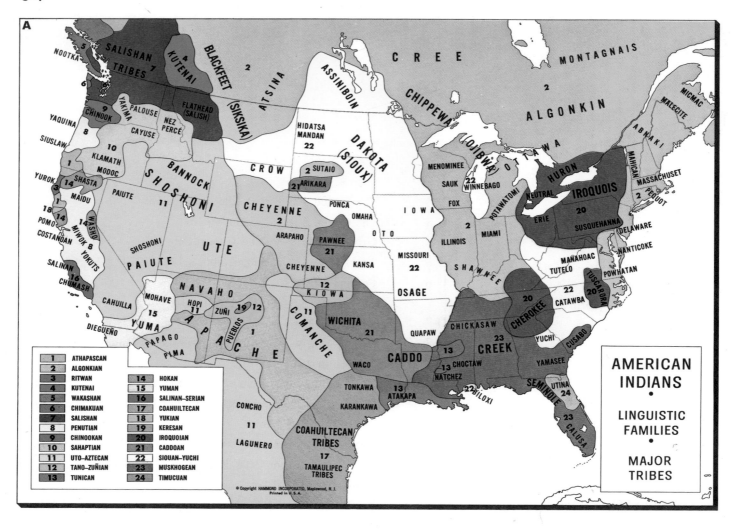

A

AMERICAN INDIANS
•
LINGUISTIC FAMILIES
•
MAJOR TRIBES

1	ATHAPASCAN	
2	ALGONKIAN	
3	RITWAN	14 HOKAN
4	KUTENAI	15 YUMAN
5	WAKASHAN	16 SALINAN–SERIAN
6	CHIMAKUAN	17 COAHUILTECAN
7	SALISHAN	18 YUKIAN
8	PENUTIAN	19 KERESAN
9	CHINOOKAN	20 IROQUOIAN
10	SAHAPTIAN	21 CADDOAN
11	UTO–AZTECAN	22 SIOUAN–YUCHI
12	TANO–ZUÑIAN	23 MUSKHOGEAN
13	TUNICAN	24 TIMUCUAN

© Copyright HAMMOND INCORPORATED, Maplewood, N. J.
Printed in U.S.A.

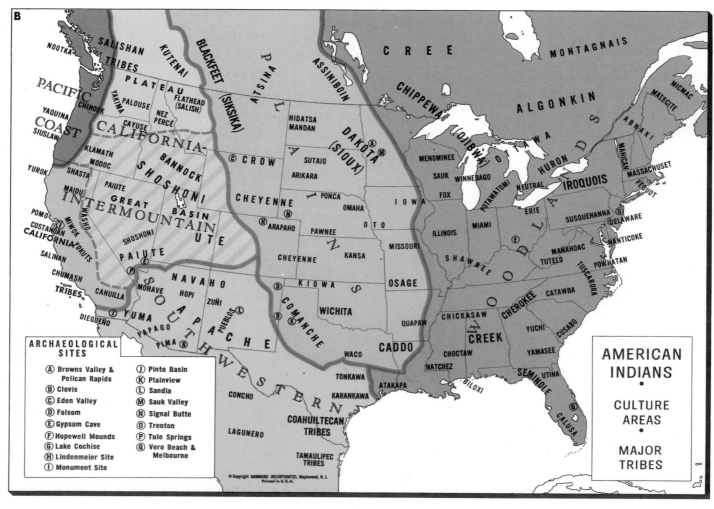

B

AMERICAN INDIANS
•
CULTURE AREAS
•
MAJOR TRIBES

ARCHAEOLOGICAL SITES

Ⓐ	Browns Valley & Pelican Rapids	Ⓙ Pinto Basin
Ⓑ	Clovis	Ⓚ Plainview
Ⓒ	Eden Valley	Ⓛ Sandia
Ⓓ	Folsom	Ⓜ Sauk Valley
Ⓔ	Gypsum Cave	Ⓝ Signal Butte
Ⓕ	Hopewell Mounds	Ⓞ Trenton
Ⓖ	Lake Cochise	Ⓟ Tule Springs
Ⓗ	Lindenmeier Site	Ⓠ Vero Beach & Melbourne
Ⓘ	Monument Site	

© Copyright HAMMOND INCORPORATED, Maplewood, N. J.
Printed in U.S.A.

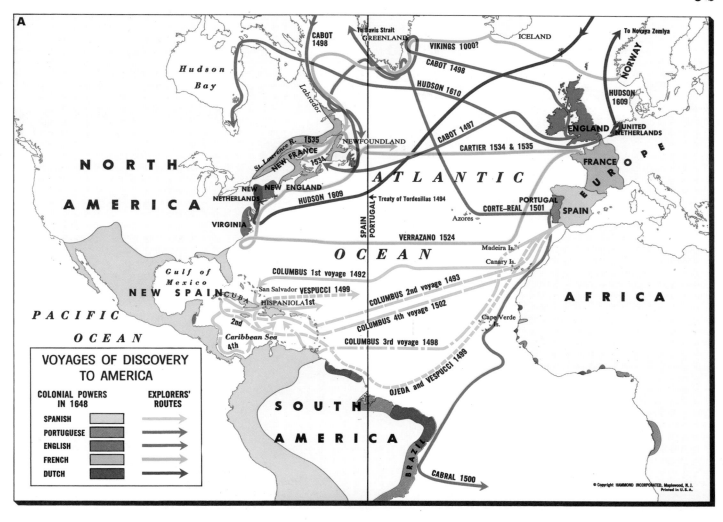

A

VOYAGES OF DISCOVERY TO AMERICA

COLONIAL POWERS IN 1648 — EXPLORERS' ROUTES

- SPANISH
- PORTUGUESE
- ENGLISH
- FRENCH
- DUTCH

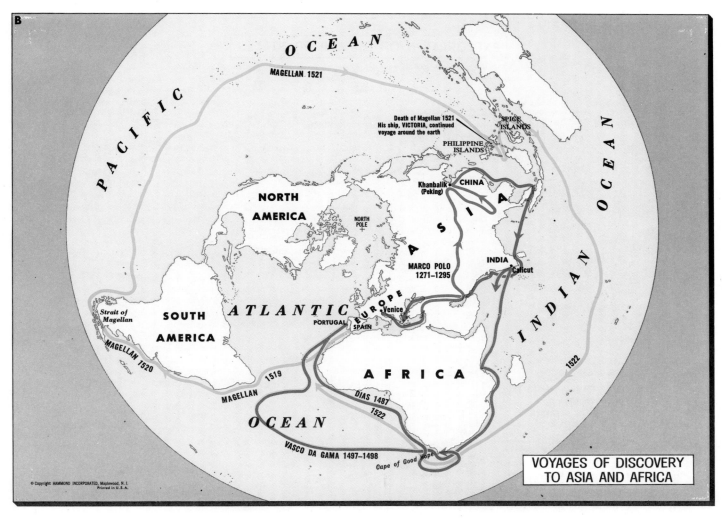

B

VOYAGES OF DISCOVERY TO ASIA AND AFRICA

A

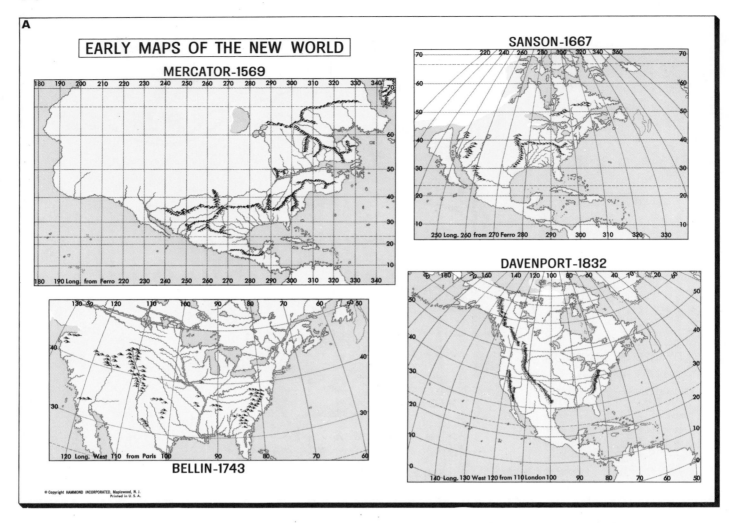

EARLY MAPS OF THE NEW WORLD
MERCATOR-1569
SANSON-1667
DAVENPORT-1832
BELLIN-1743

© Copyright HAMMOND INCORPORATED, Maplewood, N.J.
Printed in U.S.A.

B

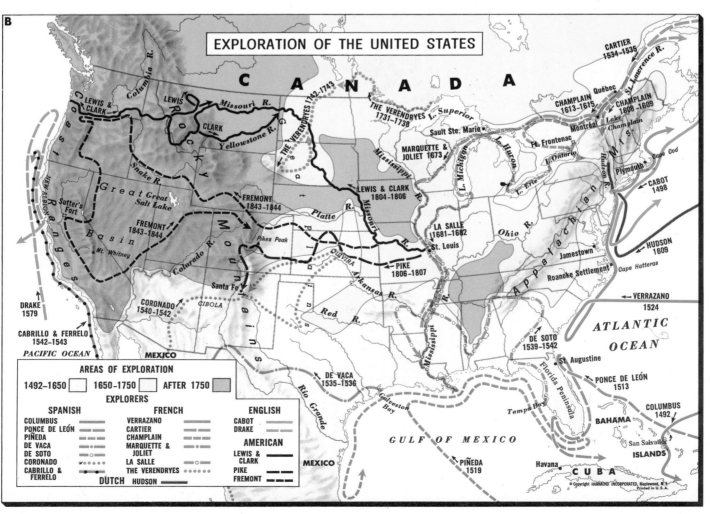

EXPLORATION OF THE UNITED STATES

AREAS OF EXPLORATION
1492–1650 1650–1750 AFTER 1750

EXPLORERS

SPANISH	FRENCH	ENGLISH
COLUMBUS	VERRAZANO	CABOT
PONCE DE LEÓN	CARTIER	DRAKE
PIÑEDA	CHAMPLAIN	
DE VACA	MARQUETTE & JOLIET	**AMERICAN**
DE SOTO		LEWIS & CLARK
CORONADO	LA SALLE	PIKE
CABRILLO & FERRELO	THE VERENDRYES	FREMONT

DUTCH HUDSON

© Copyright HAMMOND INCORPORATED, Maplewood, N.J.
Printed in U.S.A.

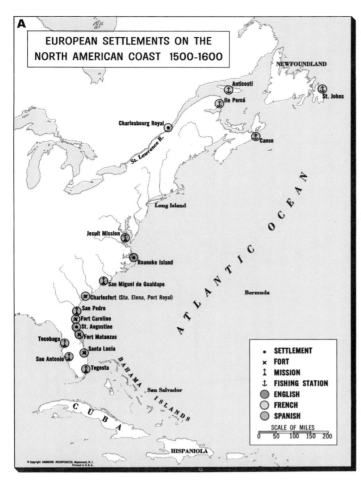

A

EUROPEAN SETTLEMENTS ON THE NORTH AMERICAN COAST 1500-1600

NEWFOUNDLAND

Anticosti
Ile Percé
St. Johns
Charlesbourg Royal
St. Lawrence R.
Canso

Long Island

Jesuit Mission

ATLANTIC OCEAN

Roanoke Island

San Miguel de Gualdape

Charlesfort (Sta. Elena, Port Royal)
San Pedro
Fort Caroline
St. Augustine
Fort Matanzas
Tocobaga
Santa Lucia
San Antonio
Tegesta

Bermuda

BAHAMA ISLANDS

San Salvador

CUBA

HISPANIOLA

● SETTLEMENT
✕ FORT
⚲ MISSION
⚲ FISHING STATION
● ENGLISH
● FRENCH
● SPANISH

SCALE OF MILES
0 50 100 150 200

© Copyright HAMMOND INCORPORATED, Maplewood, N.J.
Printed in U.S.A.

B

EUROPEAN POWERS IN THE NEW WORLD

HUDSON BAY

HUDSON'S BAY COMPANY

NEW FRANCE

NEWFOUND-LAND

ACADIA

Great Lakes
St. Lawrence R.
NEW ENGLAND

LOUISIANA

ENGLISH COLONIES

VIRGINIA

CAROLINA

Mississippi

FLORIDA

GULF OF MEXICO

CUBA

NEW SPAIN

CARIBBEAN SEA

PACIFIC OCEAN

NEW GRANADA

ATLANTIC OCEAN

ENGLISH
FRENCH
SPANISH

SCALE OF MILES
0 200 400 600

1682

© Copyright HAMMOND INCORPORATED, Maplewood, N.J.
Printed in U.S.A.

C

EUROPEAN POWERS IN THE NEW WORLD

HUDSON BAY

HUDSON'S BAY COMPANY

NEW FRANCE

NEWFOUND-LAND

ISLE ROYALE

NOVA SCOTIA

Great Lakes
St. Lawrence R.
NEW ENGLAND

LOUISIANA

ENGLISH COLONIES

VIRGINIA

CAROLINA

Mississippi

TEXAS

FLORIDA

GULF OF MEXICO

CUBA

ST. DOMINGUE (HAITI)

NEW SPAIN

CARIBBEAN SEA

PACIFIC OCEAN

NEW GRANADA

ATLANTIC OCEAN

ENGLISH
FRENCH
SPANISH

SCALE OF MILES
0 200 400 600

1713

© Copyright HAMMOND INCORPORATED, Maplewood, N.J.
Printed in U.S.A.

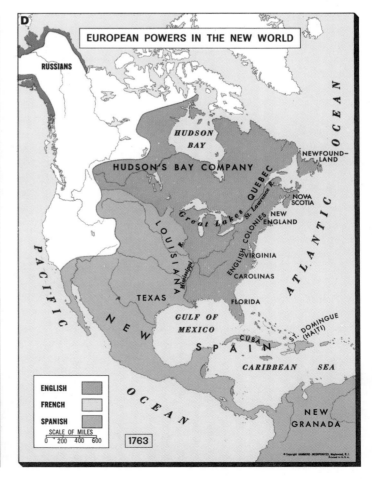

D

EUROPEAN POWERS IN THE NEW WORLD

RUSSIANS

HUDSON BAY

HUDSON'S BAY COMPANY

QUEBEC

NEWFOUND-LAND

NOVA SCOTIA

Great Lakes
St. Lawrence R.
NEW ENGLAND

LOUISIANA

ENGLISH COLONIES

VIRGINIA

CAROLINAS

Mississippi

TEXAS

FLORIDA

GULF OF MEXICO

CUBA

ST. DOMINGUE (HAITI)

NEW SPAIN

CARIBBEAN SEA

PACIFIC OCEAN

NEW GRANADA

ATLANTIC OCEAN

ENGLISH
FRENCH
SPANISH

SCALE OF MILES
0 200 400 600

1763

© Copyright HAMMOND INCORPORATED, Maplewood, N.J.
Printed in U.S.A.

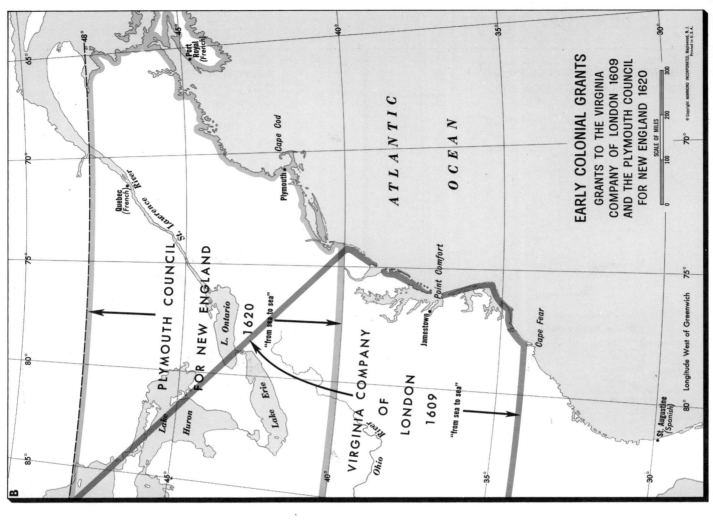

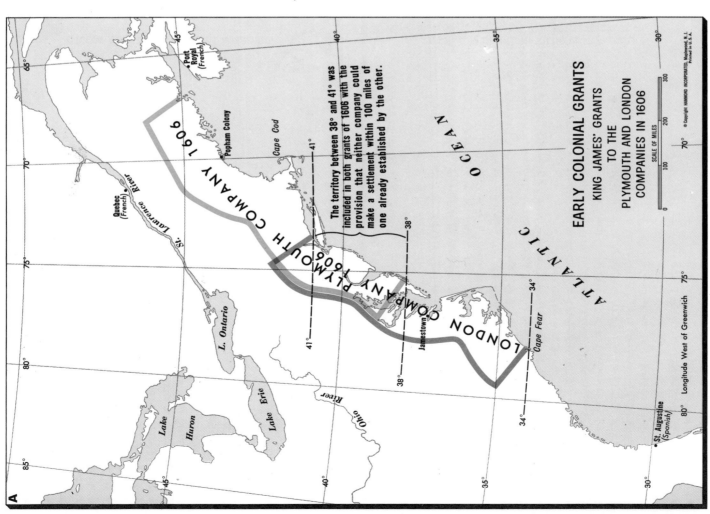

EARLY COLONIAL GRANTS
GRANTS TO THE VIRGINIA
COMPANY OF LONDON 1609
AND THE PLYMOUTH COUNCIL
FOR NEW ENGLAND 1620

SCALE OF MILES

0   100   200   300

© Copyright HAMMOND INCORPORATED, Maplewood, N.J.
Printed in U.S.A.

PLYMOUTH COUNCIL
FOR NEW ENGLAND
1620

VIRGINIA COMPANY
OF
LONDON
1609

"from sea to sea"

ATLANTIC

OCEAN

EARLY COLONIAL GRANTS
KING JAMES' GRANTS
TO THE
PLYMOUTH AND LONDON
COMPANIES IN 1606

SCALE OF MILES

0   100   200   300

© Copyright HAMMOND INCORPORATED, Maplewood, N.J.
Printed in U.S.A.

The territory between 38° and 41° was
included in both grants of 1606 with the
provision that neither company could
make a settlement within 100 miles of
one already established by the other.

PLYMOUTH COMPANY 1606

LONDON COMPANY 1606

ATLANTIC

OCEAN

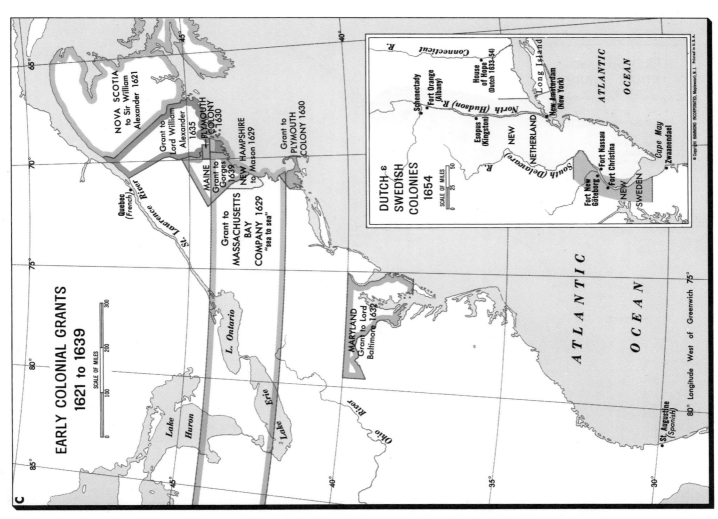

EARLY COLONIAL GRANTS 1662 to 1732

SCALE OF MILES
0 100 200 300

D

Quebec (French)

St. Lawrence River

Lake Huron

L. Ontario

Lake Erie

Ohio River

Grant to Duke of York 1664

Grant to CONNECTICUT COL. CO. 1662 "sea to sea"

Grant to Duke of York 1664

Grant to RHODE ISLAND & PROVIDENCE PLANTATIONS 1663

NEW YORK

PENNSYLVANIA
Grant to William Penn 1681

NEW JERSEY
Grant by Duke of York to Lord Berkeley & Sir George Carteret 1664

DELAWARE
Grant by Duke of York to William Penn 1682

Grant to Earl of Clarendon & others 1665 "to sea"

CAROLINA

GEORGIA
Grant to James Oglethorpe & others 1732 "sea to sea"

St. Augustine (Spanish)

ATLANTIC OCEAN

80° Longitude West of Greenwich

CONNECTICUT AND NEW HAVEN COLONIES 1635-1664 AND THE DIVISION OF NEW JERSEY 1676-1702

SCALE OF MILES
0 25 50

■ NEW HAVEN COLONY TOWNS
● CONNECTICUT COLONY TOWNS

Boundary of 1703 (New York's title confirmed 1664)

Boundary of 1662 (modified)

Hartford

CONNECTICUT COLONY

New Haven

NEW HAVEN COLONY

Boundary of 1683

Long Island (1664)

NEW YORK

Hudson R.

New York

Boundary of 1664

Boundary of 1773

Perth Amboy

EAST JERSEY

WEST JERSEY

Burlington

Philadelphia

PENNSYLVANIA

Delaware R.

Delaware Bay

Cape May

© Copyright HAMMOND INCORPORATED, Maplewood, N.J. Printed in U.S.A.

EARLY COLONIAL GRANTS 1621 to 1639

SCALE OF MILES
0 100 200 300

C

Quebec (French)

St. Lawrence River

Lake Huron

L. Ontario

Lake Erie

Ohio River

NOVA SCOTIA to Sir William Alexander 1621

Grant to Lord William Alexander 1635

PLYMOUTH COLONY 1630

MAINE Grant to Gorges 1639

NEW HAMPSHIRE to Mason 1629

Grant to MASSACHUSETTS BAY COMPANY 1629 "sea to sea"

Grant to PLYMOUTH COLONY 1630

MARYLAND Grant to Lord Baltimore 1632

St. Augustine (Spanish)

ATLANTIC OCEAN

80° Longitude West of Greenwich 75°

DUTCH & SWEDISH COLONIES 1654

SCALE OF MILES
0 25 50

Connecticut R.

Schenectady

Fort Orange (Albany)

House of Hope (Dutch 1633-54)

Esopus (Kingston)

North (Hudson) R.

NEW NETHERLAND

Long Island

New Amsterdam (New York)

ATLANTIC OCEAN

Cape May

South (Delaware) R.

Fort New Göteborg

Fort Christina

Fort Nassau

NEW SWEDEN

Zwaanendael

© Copyright HAMMOND INCORPORATED, Maplewood, N.J. Printed in U.S.A.

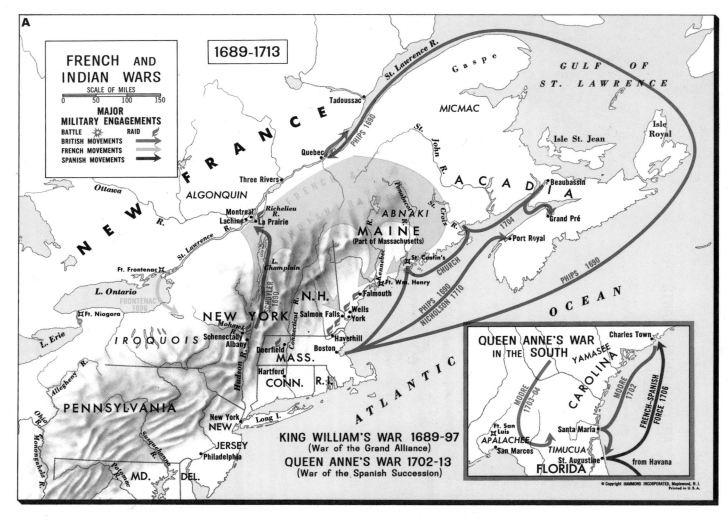

A

1689-1713

FRENCH AND
INDIAN WARS
SCALE OF MILES
0   50   100   150
MAJOR
MILITARY ENGAGEMENTS
BATTLE ☼   RAID
BRITISH MOVEMENTS
FRENCH MOVEMENTS
SPANISH MOVEMENTS

KING WILLIAM'S WAR 1689-97
(War of the Grand Alliance)
QUEEN ANNE'S WAR 1702-13
(War of the Spanish Succession)

QUEEN ANNE'S WAR
IN THE SOUTH

© Copyright HAMMOND INCORPORATED, Maplewood, N.J.
Printed in U.S.A.

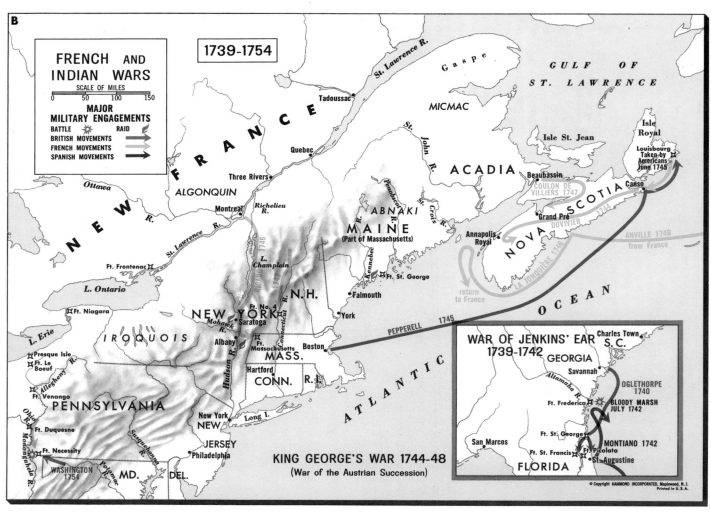

B

1739-1754

FRENCH AND
INDIAN WARS
SCALE OF MILES
0   50   100   150
MAJOR
MILITARY ENGAGEMENTS
BATTLE ☼   RAID
BRITISH MOVEMENTS
FRENCH MOVEMENTS
SPANISH MOVEMENTS

KING GEORGE'S WAR 1744-48
(War of the Austrian Succession)

WAR OF JENKINS' EAR
1739-1742

© Copyright HAMMOND INCORPORATED, Maplewood, N.J.
Printed in U.S.A.

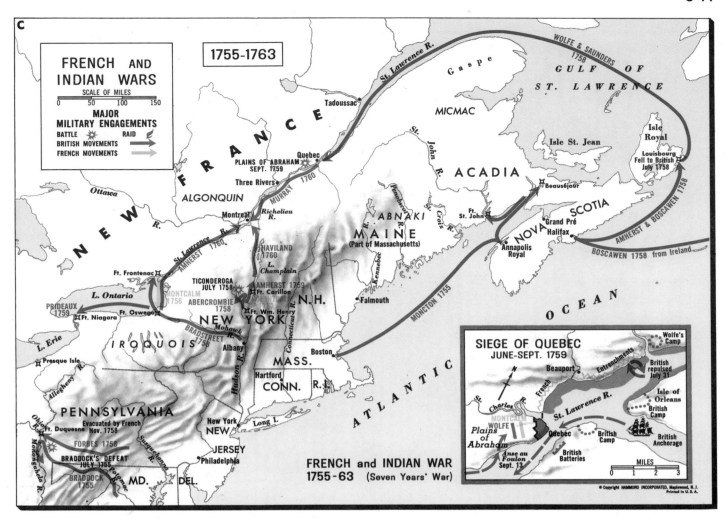

C

FRENCH AND INDIAN WARS

1755-1763

SCALE OF MILES
0   50   100   150

MAJOR MILITARY ENGAGEMENTS
- BATTLE
- RAID
- BRITISH MOVEMENTS
- FRENCH MOVEMENTS

NEW FRANCE

St. Lawrence R.

Gaspe

GULF OF ST. LAWRENCE

WOLFE & SAUNDERS 1758

Tadoussac

MICMAC

Isle St. Jean

Isle Royal

Louisbourg Fell to British July 1758

St. John R.

ACADIA

AMHERST & BOSCAWEN 1758

PLAINS OF ABRAHAM SEPT. 1759

Quebec

Three Rivers

MURRAY 1760

ALGONQUIN

Montreal

Richelieu R.

ABNAKI

Beauséjour

Ft. St. John

NOVA SCOTIA

Grand Pré

Halifax

BOSCAWEN 1758 from Ireland

St. Croix R.

MAINE (Part of Massachusetts)

Annapolis Royal

St. Lawrence 1760

AMHERST 1760

HAVILAND 1760

L. Champlain

Kennebec R.

MONCTON 1755

Ft. Frontenac

TICONDEROGA JULY 1758

AMHERST 1759

Ft. Carillon

N.H.

MONTCALM 1756

ABERCROMBIE 1758

Falmouth

ATLANTIC OCEAN

PRIDEAUX 1759

L. Ontario

Ft. Niagara

Ft. Oswego

NEW YORK

Ft. Wm. Henry

BRADSTREET 1758

Mohawk R.

Albany

Boston

L. Erie

IROQUOIS

MASS.

Presque Isle

Hudson R.

Hartford

CONN. R.

Allegheny R.

Ohio R.

PENNSYLVANIA

Evacuated by French Nov. 1758

Ft. Duquesne

New York

Long I.

NEW JERSEY

Monongahela R.

FORBES 1758

Susquehanna R.

Philadelphia

BRADDOCK'S DEFEAT JULY 1755

BRADDOCK 1755

MD.

DEL.

Potomac R.

SIEGE OF QUEBEC
JUNE-SEPT. 1759

Wolfe's Camp

Beauport

Entrenchments

British repulsed July 31

St. Charles R.

French

St. Lawrence R.

Isle of Orleans

British Camp

MONTCALM

WOLFE

Plains of Abraham

Quebec

Anse au Foulon Sept. 13

British Batteries

British Camp

British Anchorage

MILES
0   1   2   3

FRENCH and INDIAN WAR
1755-63 (Seven Years' War)

© Copyright HAMMOND INCORPORATED, Maplewood, N.J.
Printed in U.S.A.

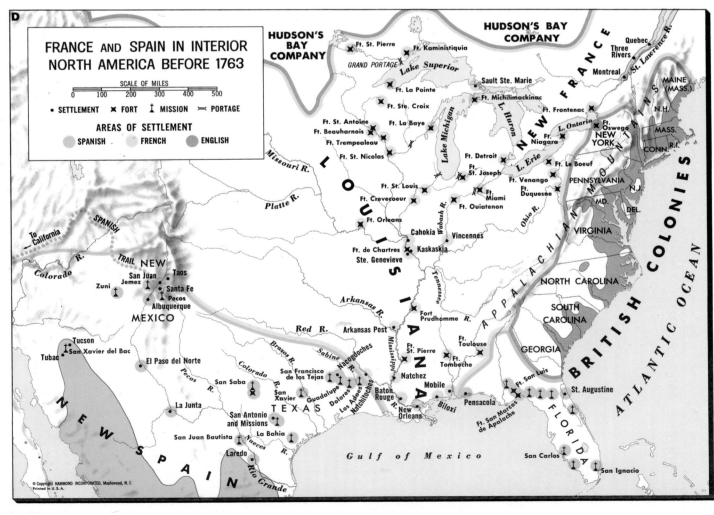

D

FRANCE AND SPAIN IN INTERIOR NORTH AMERICA BEFORE 1763

SCALE OF MILES
0   100   200   300   400   500

- • SETTLEMENT
- ✕ FORT
- ⊥ MISSION
- ⋈ PORTAGE

AREAS OF SETTLEMENT
- ○ SPANISH
- ○ FRENCH
- ○ ENGLISH

HUDSON'S BAY COMPANY

HUDSON'S BAY COMPANY

Ft. St. Pierre

Ft. Kaministiquia

GRAND PORTAGE

Lake Superior

Quebec

Three Rivers

St. Lawrence R.

Montreal

NEW FRANCE

Ft. La Pointe

Sault Ste. Marie

Ft. Michilimackinac

MAINE (MASS.)

N.H.

Ft. Ste. Croix

Ft. St. Antoine

Ft. Beauharnois

Ft. La Baye

L. Huron

Ft. Frontenac

L. Ontario

Ft. Oswego

MASS.

Ft. Trempealeau

Lake Michigan

Ft. Niagara

NEW YORK

CONN. R.I.

Ft. St. Nicolas

Ft. Detroit

L. Erie

Ft. Le Boeuf

Missouri R.

Ft. St. Joseph

Ft. Venango

PENNSYLVANIA

N.J.

LOUISIANA

Ft. St. Louis

Ft. Miami

Ft. Duquesne

MD.

DEL.

Platte R.

Ft. Crevecoeur

Wabash R.

Ft. Ouiatenon

Ohio R.

VIRGINIA

SPANISH

Ft. Orleans

Cahokia

Vincennes

APPALACHIAN MOUNTAINS

To California

TRAIL

NEW

Ft. de Chartres

Kaskaskia

Ste. Genevieve

Colorado R.

Taos

San Juan

Jemez

Zuni

Santa Fe

Pecos

Albuquerque

Tennessee R.

NORTH CAROLINA

MEXICO

Arkansas R.

SOUTH CAROLINA

Fort Prudhomme R.

BRITISH COLONIES

Tucson

San Xavier del Bac

Tubac

Red R.

Arkansas Post

Ft. Toulouse

GEORGIA

ATLANTIC OCEAN

El Paso del Norte

Pecos R.

Brazos R.

Sabine R.

Nacogdoches

Ft. St. Pierre

Ft. Tombeche

Ft. San Luis

St. Augustine

Colorado R.

San Francisco de los Tejas

Natchez

San Saba

San Xavier

Guadalupe

Dolores

Los Adaes

Natchitoches

Baton Rouge

Mobile

Biloxi

Pensacola

FLORIDA

La Junta

TEXAS

Mississippi R.

New Orleans

Ft. San Marcos de Apalache

San Antonio and Missions

San Juan Bautista

La Bahia

Nueces R.

Laredo

Rio Grande

Gulf of Mexico

San Carlos

San Ignacio

NEW SPAIN

© Copyright HAMMOND INCORPORATED, Maplewood, N.J.
Printed in U.S.A.

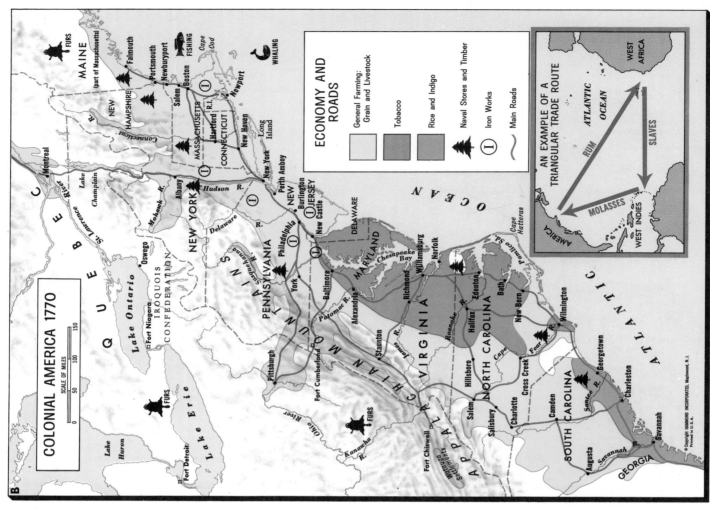

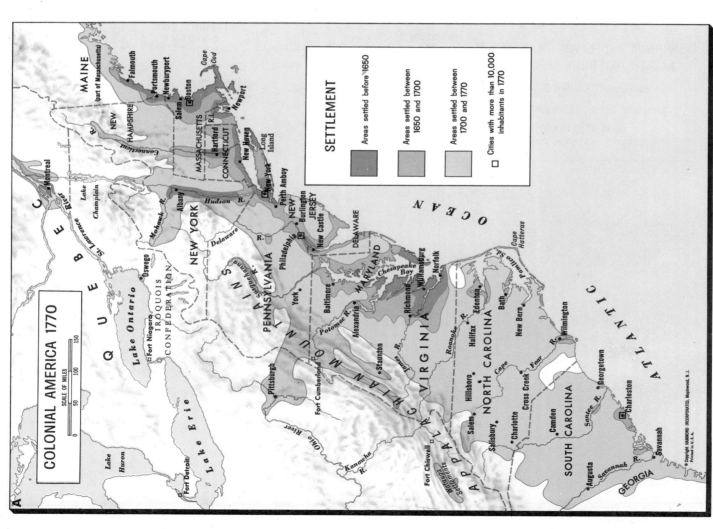

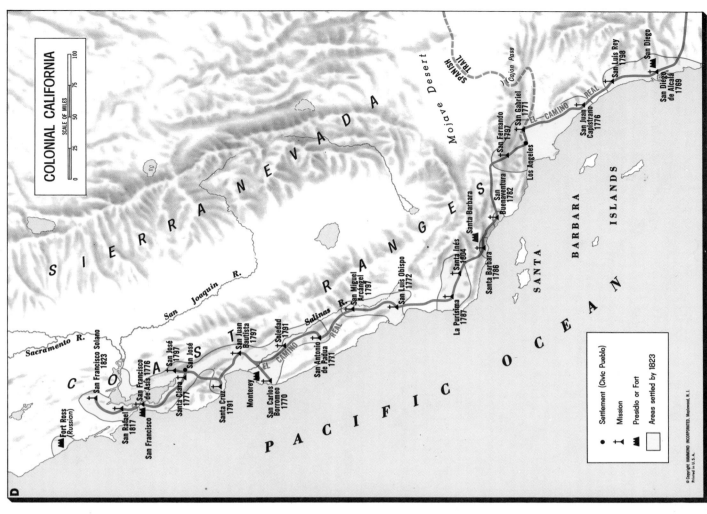

COLONIAL CALIFORNIA

SCALE OF MILES
0 25 50 75 100

Fort Ross (Russian)

San Rafael 1817
San Francisco Solano 1823
San Francisco de Asís 1776
San Francisco
San José 1797
San José
Santa Clara 1777
Santa Cruz 1791
San Juan Bautista 1797
Soledad 1791
Monterey
San Carlos Borromeo 1770
San Antonio de Padua 1771
San Miguel Arcángel 1797
San Luis Obispo 1772
La Purísima 1787
Santa Inés 1804
Santa Bárbara 1786
Santa Bárbara
San Buenaventura 1782
San Fernando 1797
San Gabriel 1771
Los Angeles
San Juan Capistrano 1776
San Luis Rey 1798
San Diego
San Diego de Alcalá 1769

SIERRA NEVADA
COAST RANGES
Sacramento R.
San Joaquin R.
Salinas R.
Mojave Desert
SPANISH TRAIL
Cajon Pass
EL CAMINO REAL

PACIFIC OCEAN
SANTA BARBARA ISLANDS

● Settlement (Civic Pueblo)
⊥ Mission
▲ Presidio or Fort
☐ Areas settled by 1823

© Copyright HAMMOND INCORPORATED, Maplewood, N.J.
Printed in U.S.A.

D

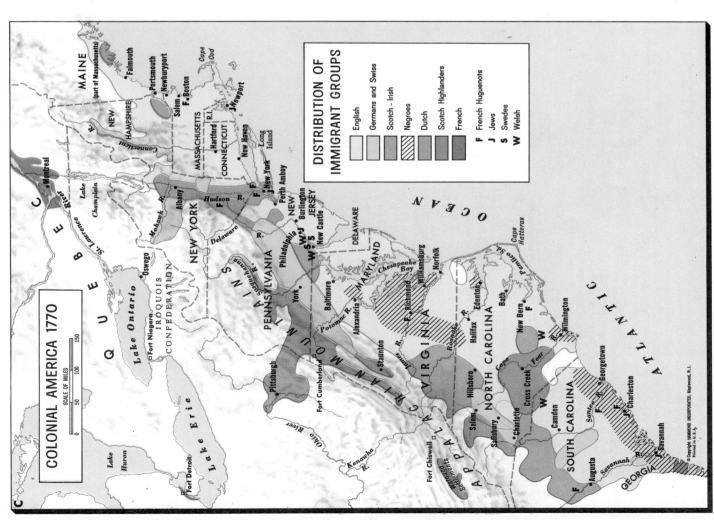

COLONIAL AMERICA 1770

SCALE OF MILES
0 50 100 150

DISTRIBUTION OF IMMIGRANT GROUPS

English
Germans and Swiss
Scotch - Irish
Negroes
Dutch
Scotch Highlanders
French

F French Huguenots
J Jews
S Swedes
W Welsh

QUEBEC
Montreal
St. Lawrence River
Lake Champlain
Lake Huron
Lake Ontario
Lake Erie
Fort Detroit
Fort Niagara
Oswego
IROQUOIS CONFEDERATION
Ohio River
Kanawha R.
Fort Chiswell
Fort Cumberland
Pittsburgh

MAINE (part of Massachusetts)
Falmouth
Portsmouth
Newburyport
NEW HAMPSHIRE
Salem
F. Boston
Cape Cod
MASSACHUSETTS
Hartford
CONNECTICUT
New Haven
R.I.
Newport
Long Island
New York
Perth Amboy
Albany
Mohawk R.
Hudson R.
Delaware R.
NEW YORK
NEW JERSEY
Burlington
New Castle
Philadelphia
PENNSYLVANIA
Susquehanna R.
York
Baltimore
DELAWARE
MARYLAND
Alexandria
Potomac R.
Williamsburg
Richmond
VIRGINIA
James R.
Norfolk
Chesapeake Bay
Cape Hatteras
Pamlico Sd.
Edenton
Bath
New Bern
NORTH CAROLINA
Roanoke R.
Halifax
Hillsboro
Salem
Salisbury
Charlotte
Staunton
Cross Creek
Cape Fear R.
Wilmington
Camden
SOUTH CAROLINA
Charleston
Georgetown
Santee R.
Augusta
Savannah R.
GEORGIA
Savannah
APPALACHIAN MOUNTAINS
ATLANTIC OCEAN

© Copyright HAMMOND INCORPORATED, Maplewood, N.J.
Printed in U.S.A.

C

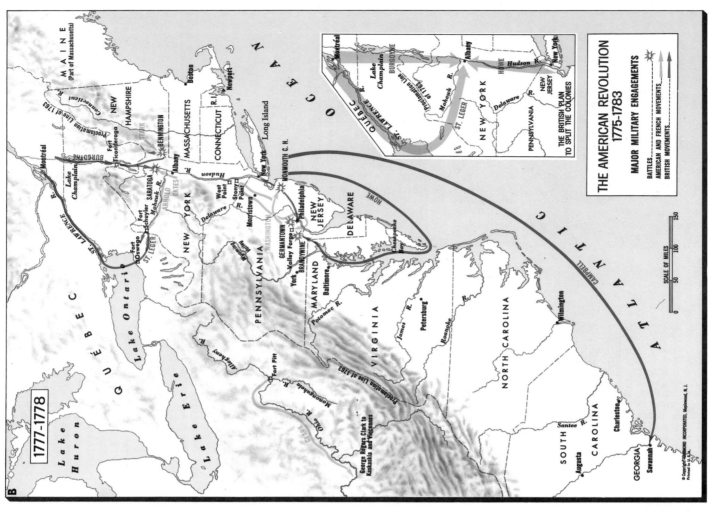

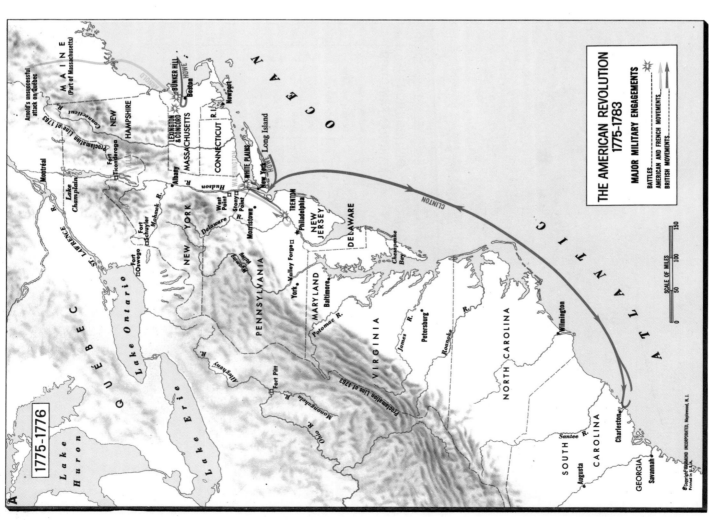

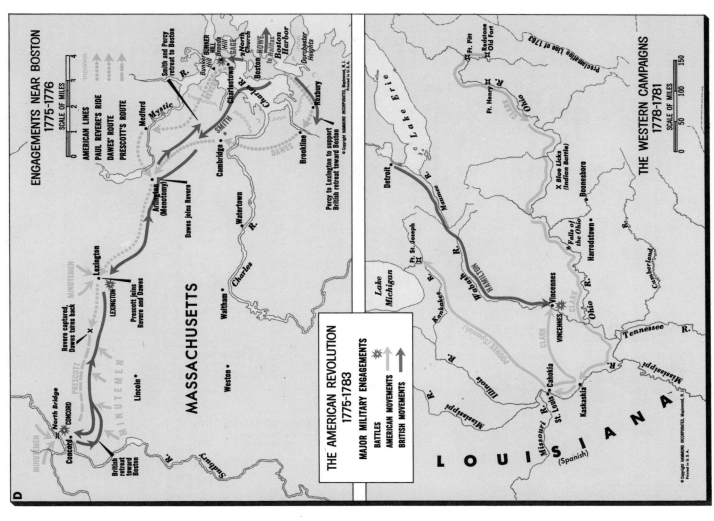

ENGAGEMENTS NEAR BOSTON 1775-1776

SCALE OF MILES
0 1 2 3 4

AMERICAN LINES
PAUL REVERE'S RIDE
DAWES' ROUTE
PRESCOTT'S ROUTE

© Copyright HAMMOND INCORPORATED, Maplewood, N.J. Printed in U.S.A.

Smith and Percy retreat to Boston
BUNKER HILL
North Church
GAGE
HOWE to Halifax
Boston Harbor
Dorchester Heights
Boston
Charlestown
Roxbury
Brookline
SMITH
Medford
Cambridge
Watertown
Waltham
Weston
Charles R.
MASSACHUSETTS
Lexington
Prescott joins Revere and Dawes
Revere captured, Dawes turns back
Arlington (Menotomy)
Dawes joins Revere
Percy to Lexington to support British retreat toward Boston
MINUTEMEN
PRESCOTT
Lincoln
North Bridge
CONCORD
British retreat toward Boston
Concord
Sudbury R.

THE AMERICAN REVOLUTION 1775-1783
MAJOR MILITARY ENGAGEMENTS
BATTLES
AMERICAN MOVEMENTS
BRITISH MOVEMENTS

THE WESTERN CAMPAIGNS 1778-1781

SCALE OF MILES
0 50 100 150

© Copyright HAMMOND INCORPORATED, Maplewood, N.J. Printed in U.S.A.

Lake Erie
Detroit
Ft. Pitt
Redstone Old Fort
Proclamation Line of 1763
Ft. Henry
Ohio R.
CLARK
Maumee R.
HAMILTON
Wabash R.
Lake Michigan
Ft. St. Joseph
Blue Licks (Indian Battle)
Boonesboro
Falls of the Ohio
Harrodstown
Cumberland R.
Vincennes
VINCENNES
CLARK
Ohio R.
Tennessee R.
Kaskaskia
Cahokia
St. Louis
POUVER (Spanish)
Illinois R.
Missouri R.
Mississippi R.
LOUISIANA (Spanish)

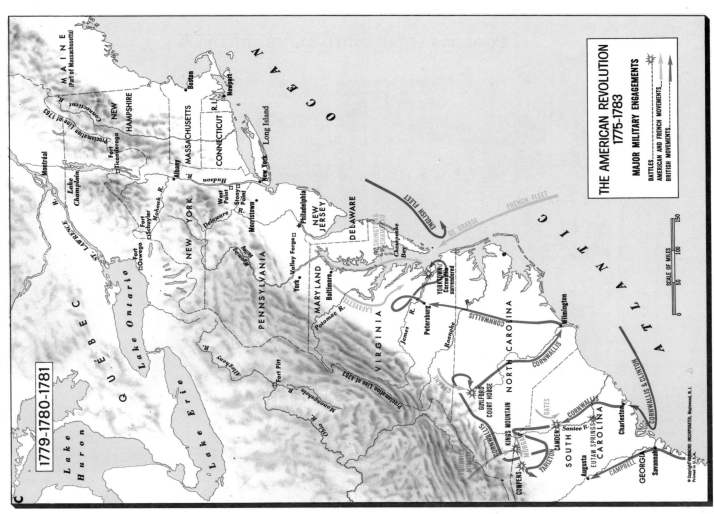

THE AMERICAN REVOLUTION 1775-1783
MAJOR MILITARY ENGAGEMENTS
BATTLES
AMERICAN AND FRENCH MOVEMENTS
BRITISH MOVEMENTS

1779-1780-1781

SCALE OF MILES
0 50 100 150

© Copyright HAMMOND INCORPORATED, Maplewood, N.J. Printed in U.S.A.

MAINE (Part of Massachusetts)
NEW HAMPSHIRE
Boston
MASSACHUSETTS
R.I.
Newport
CONNECTICUT
Long Island
New York
Proclamation Line of 1763
Connecticut R.
Fort Ticonderoga
Lake Champlain
Montreal
St. Lawrence R.
QUEBEC
Lake Ontario
Fort Oswego
Lake Erie
Lake Huron
Albany
Hudson R.
Mohawk R.
Fort Schuyler
West Point
Stony Point
NEW YORK
NEW JERSEY
Morristown
Valley Forge
Delaware R.
PENNSYLVANIA
York
Philadelphia
DELAWARE
MARYLAND
Baltimore
Fort Pitt
Monongahela R.
Alleghany R.
Ohio R.
Proclamation Line of 1763
WASHINGTON
ROCHAMBEAU
Chesapeake Bay
Potomac R.
ENGLISH FLEET
DE GRASSE
FRENCH FLEET
LAFAYETTE
VIRGINIA
James R.
Petersburg
Roanoke R.
YORKTOWN Cornwallis surrendered
Wilmington
CORNWALLIS
NORTH CAROLINA
GUILFORD COURT HOUSE
GREENE
GATES
Kings Mountain
MORGAN
Cowpens
TARLETON
Camden
Santee R.
Eutaw Springs
SOUTH CAROLINA
Charleston
Augusta
Savannah
GEORGIA
CAMPBELL
CLINTON
CORNWALLIS & CLINTON
ATLANTIC OCEAN

THE AMERICAN REVOLUTION 1775-1783
MAJOR MILITARY ENGAGEMENTS
BATTLES
AMERICAN AND FRENCH MOVEMENTS
BRITISH MOVEMENTS

A

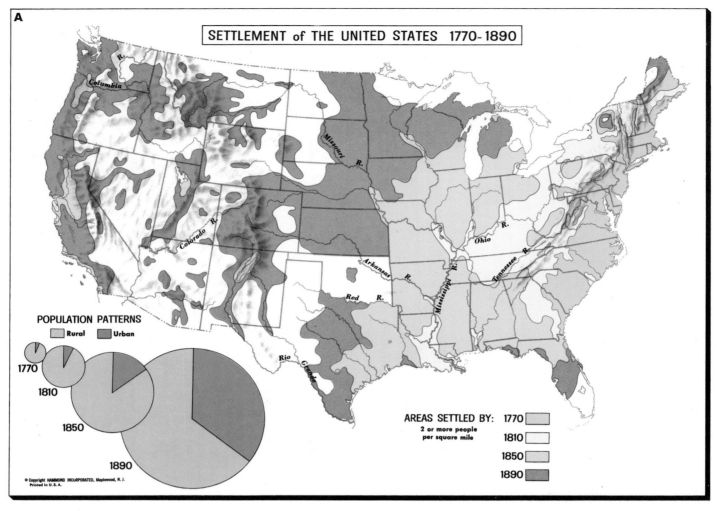

SETTLEMENT of THE UNITED STATES 1770-1890

POPULATION PATTERNS

Rural Urban

1770
1810
1850
1890

AREAS SETTLED BY:
2 or more people
per square mile

1770
1810
1850
1890

© Copyright HAMMOND INCORPORATED, Maplewood, N. J.
Printed in U.S.A.

B

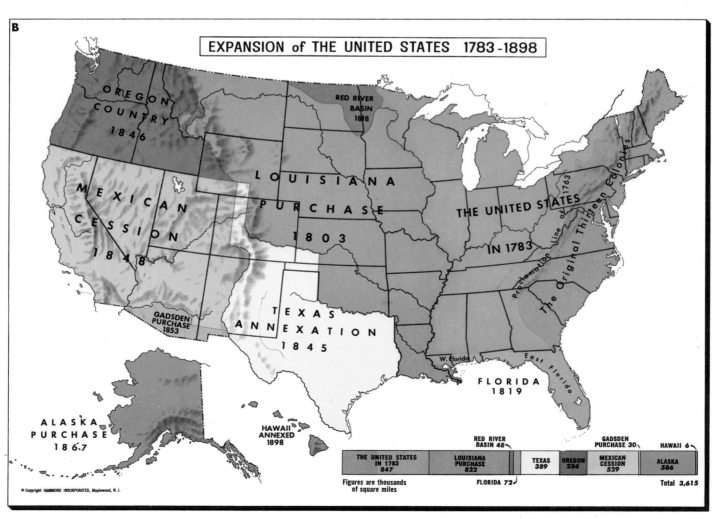

EXPANSION of THE UNITED STATES 1783-1898

OREGON COUNTRY 1846

RED RIVER BASIN 1818

MEXICAN CESSION 1848

LOUISIANA PURCHASE 1803

THE UNITED STATES IN 1783

Proclamation Line of 1763

The Original Thirteen Colonies

GADSDEN PURCHASE 1853

TEXAS ANNEXATION 1845

W. Florida

East Florida

FLORIDA 1819

ALASKA PURCHASE 1867

HAWAII ANNEXED 1898

THE UNITED STATES IN 1783 847	LOUISIANA PURCHASE 822	TEXAS 389	OREGON 286	MEXICAN CESSION 529	ALASKA 586

RED RIVER BASIN 48
GADSDEN PURCHASE 30
HAWAII 6

Figures are thousands of square miles

FLORIDA 72

Total 3,615

© Copyright HAMMOND INCORPORATED, Maplewood, N. J.

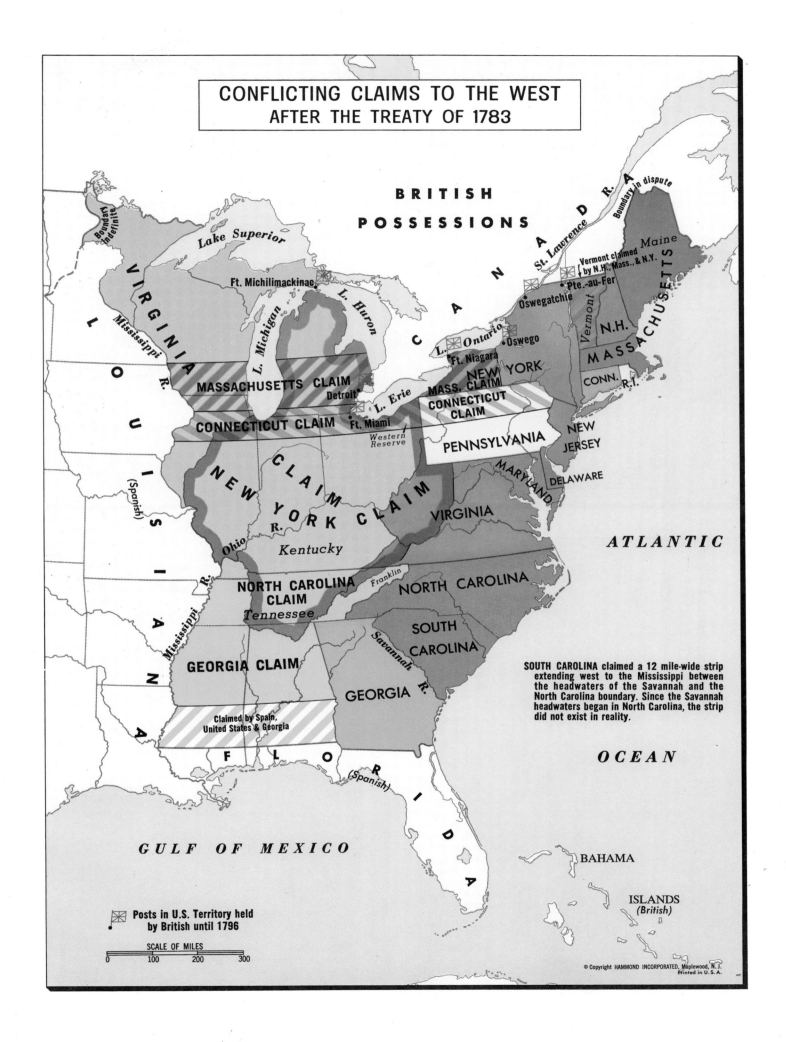

CONFLICTING CLAIMS TO THE WEST
AFTER THE TREATY OF 1783

BRITISH POSSESSIONS

CANADA

Boundary in dispute

Lake Superior

St. Lawrence R.

Maine

Vermont claimed by N.H., Mass., & N.Y.

Ft. Michilimackinac

L. Huron

Oswegatchie

Pte.-au-Fer

Vermont

N.H.

VIRGINIA

L. Michigan

L. Ontario

Oswego

Ft. Niagara

MASSACHUSETTS

LOUISIANA

Mississippi R.

MASSACHUSETTS CLAIM

Detroit

L. Erie

MASS. CLAIM

CONNECTICUT CLAIM

NEW YORK

CONN.

R.I.

CONNECTICUT CLAIM

Ft. Miami

Western Reserve

PENNSYLVANIA

NEW JERSEY

(Spanish)

NEW YORK CLAIM

MARYLAND

DELAWARE

Ohio R.

Kentucky

VIRGINIA

ATLANTIC

NORTH CAROLINA CLAIM

Franklin

Tennessee

NORTH CAROLINA

GEORGIA CLAIM

SOUTH CAROLINA

Savannah R.

GEORGIA

Mississippi R.

SOUTH CAROLINA claimed a 12 mile-wide strip extending west to the Mississippi between the headwaters of the Savannah and the North Carolina boundary. Since the Savannah headwaters began in North Carolina, the strip did not exist in reality.

Claimed by Spain, United States & Georgia

OCEAN

FLORIDA

(Spanish)

GULF OF MEXICO

BAHAMA

ISLANDS (British)

⊠ Posts in U.S. Territory held by British until 1796

SCALE OF MILES
0   100   200   300

© Copyright HAMMOND INCORPORATED, Maplewood, N.J.
Printed in U.S.A.

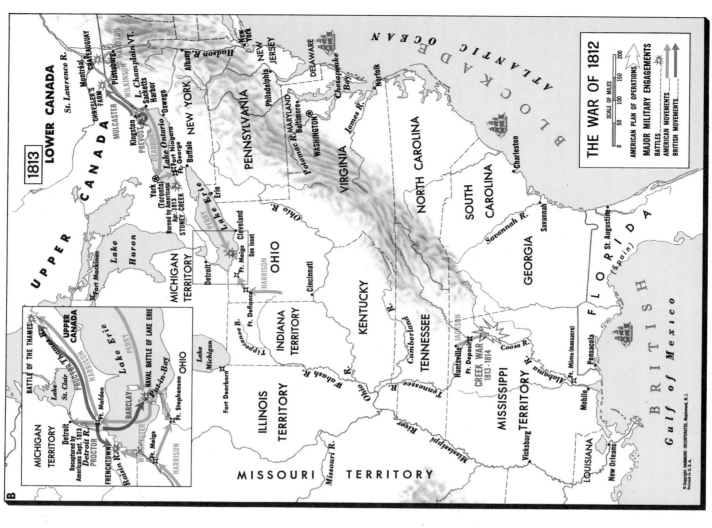

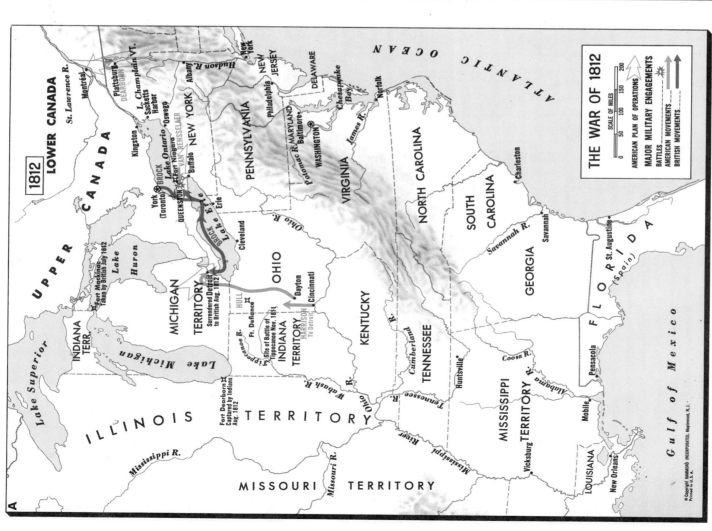

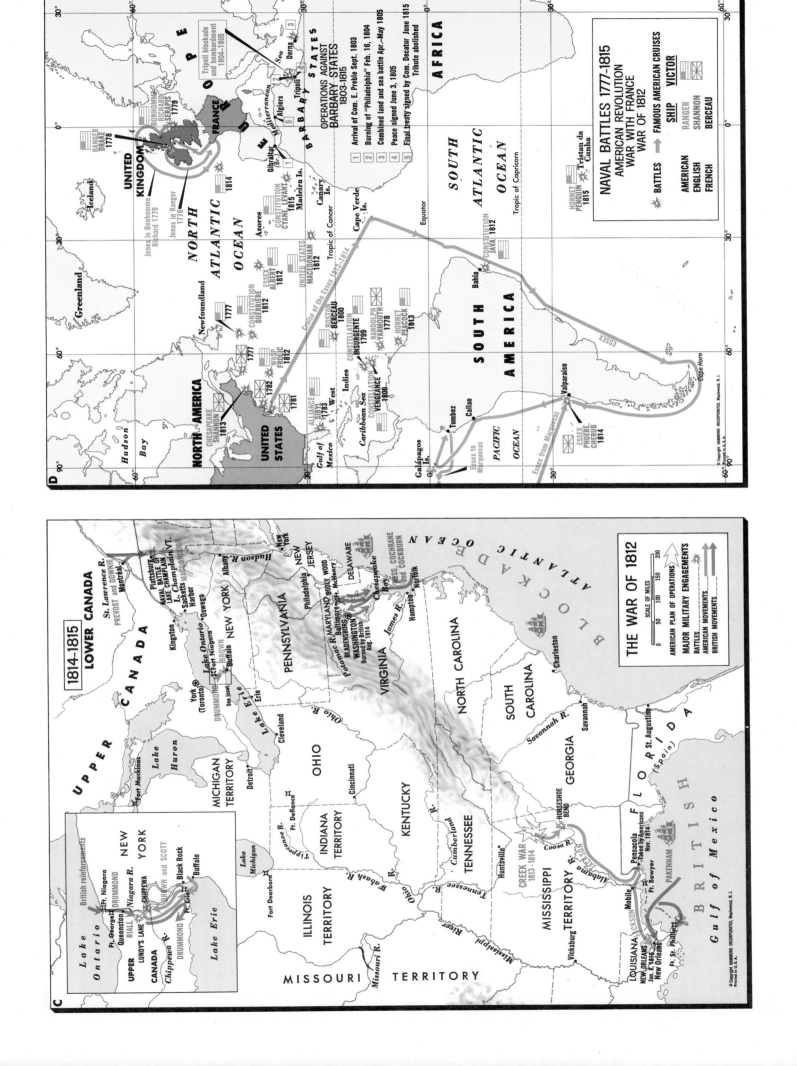

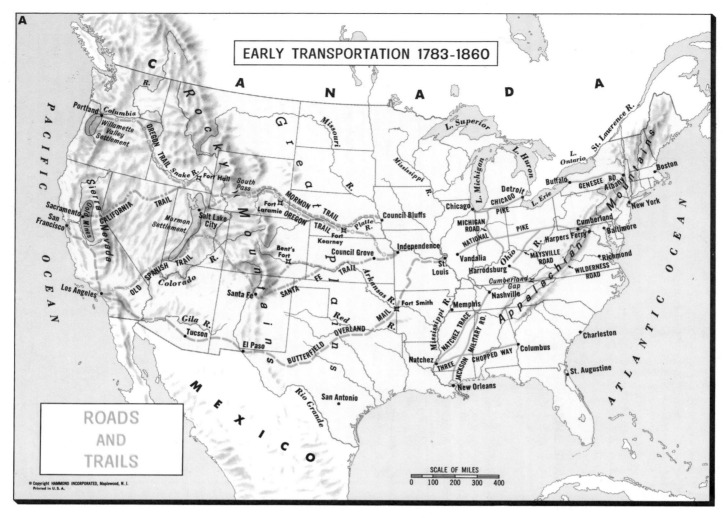

EARLY TRANSPORTATION 1783-1860

ROADS
AND
TRAILS

© Copyright HAMMOND INCORPORATED, Maplewood, N. J.
Printed in U.S.A.

SCALE OF MILES
0   100   200   300   400

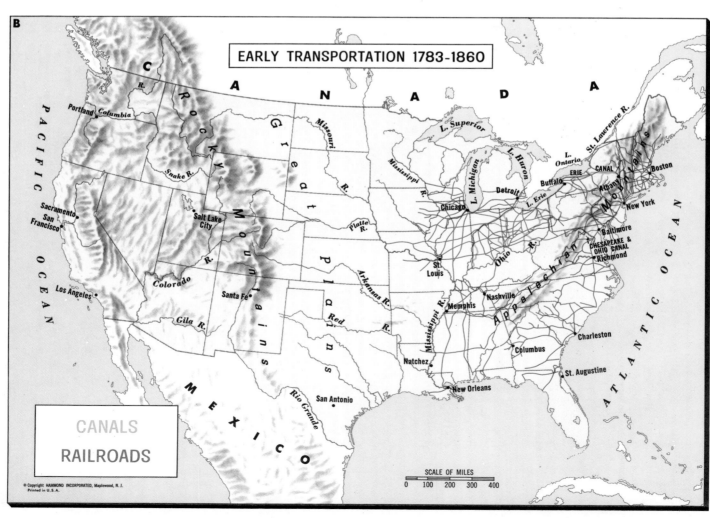

EARLY TRANSPORTATION 1783-1860

CANALS
RAILROADS

© Copyright HAMMOND INCORPORATED, Maplewood, N. J.
Printed in U.S.A.

SCALE OF MILES
0   100   200   300   400

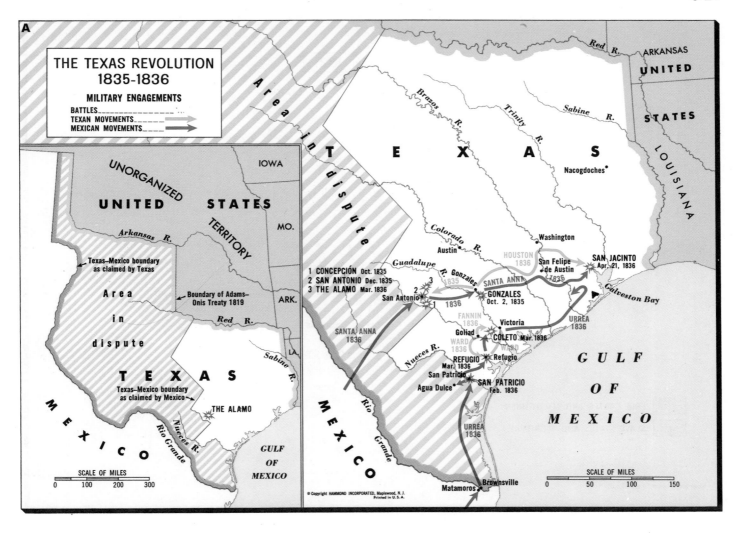

A

THE TEXAS REVOLUTION 1835-1836

MILITARY ENGAGEMENTS

BATTLES............................
TEXAN MOVEMENTS.............
MEXICAN MOVEMENTS..........

UNORGANIZED

UNITED STATES TERRITORY

IOWA

Arkansas R.

MO.

Texas–Mexico boundary as claimed by Texas

Boundary of Adams–Onis Treaty 1819

A r e a

ARK.

Red R.

i n

Sabine R.

dispute

LA.

T E X A S

Texas–Mexico boundary as claimed by Mexico

M E X I C O

THE ALAMO

Rio Grande

Nueces R.

GULF OF MEXICO

SCALE OF MILES
0   100   200   300

ARKANSAS

UNITED

Red R.

STATES

T E X A S

Brazos R.

Trinity R.

Sabine R.

LOUISIANA

Nacogdoches

A r e a   i n   d i s p u t e

Colorado R.

Austin

Washington

HOUSTON 1836

San Felipe de Austin

SAN JACINTO Apr. 21, 1836

1 CONCEPCIÓN Oct. 1835
2 SAN ANTONIO Dec. 1835
3 THE ALAMO Mar. 1836

Guadalupe R.

Gonzales

SANTA ANNA 1836

2 3
1
San Antonio

GONZALES Oct. 2, 1835

1836

Calveston Bay

URREA 1836

SANTA ANNA 1836

FANNIN 1836

Victoria

WARD 1836

COLETO Mar. 1836

Nueces R.

Goliad

WARD 1836

REFUGIO Mar. 1836

San Patricio

Refugio

SAN PATRICIO Feb. 1836

Agua Dulce

GULF

OF

MEXICO

URREA 1836

M E X I C O

Rio Grande

Matamoros

Brownsville

SCALE OF MILES
0   50   100   150

© Copyright HAMMOND INCORPORATED, Maplewood, N.J.
Printed in U.S.A.

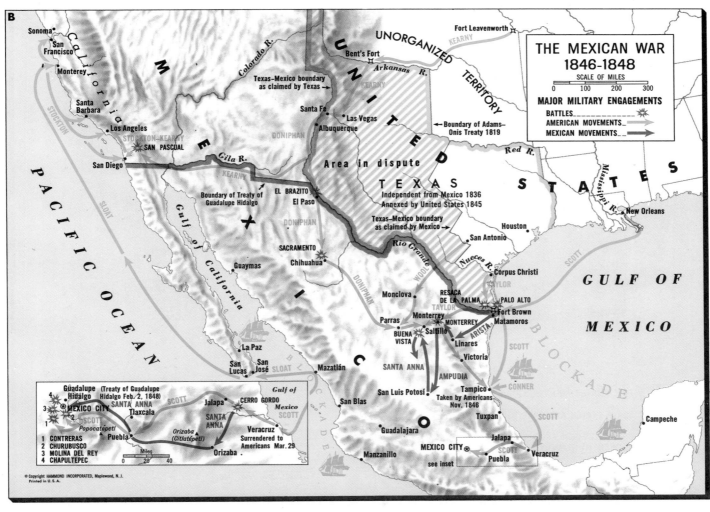

B

Sonoma

San Francisco

California

Monterey

Santa Barbara

Los Angeles

PACIFIC OCEAN

STOCKTON–KEARNY

SAN PASCUAL

San Diego

Gila R.

KEARNY

Boundary of Treaty of Guadalupe Hidalgo

Gulf of California

Guaymas

M E X I C O

SACRAMENTO

Chihuahua

DONIPHAN

La Paz

San Lucas

San José

SLOAT

Mazatlán

San Blas

Guadalajara

Manzanillo

Fort Leavenworth

KEARNY

UNORGANIZED

TERRITORY

Bent's Fort

Arkansas R.

U N I T E D

KEARNY

Texas–Mexico boundary as claimed by Texas

Santa Fe

Las Vegas

Albuquerque

DONIPHAN

EL BRAZITO
El Paso

Boundary of Adams–Onis Treaty 1819

S T A T E S

Red R.

Area in dispute

T E X A S

Independent from Mexico 1836
Annexed by United States 1845

Texas–Mexico boundary as claimed by Mexico

Rio Grande

Nueces R.

Houston

San Antonio

Corpus Christi

THE MEXICAN WAR 1846-1848

SCALE OF MILES
0   100   200   300

MAJOR MILITARY ENGAGEMENTS

BATTLES..........................
AMERICAN MOVEMENTS........
MEXICAN MOVEMENTS..........

Mississippi R.

New Orleans

GULF OF

MEXICO

BLOCKADE

SCOTT

CONNER

DONIPHAN

Monclova

Parras

RESACA DE LA PALMA

TAYLOR

Monterrey

MONTERREY

PALO ALTO

Fort Brown

Matamoros

BUENA VISTA

Saltillo

ARISTA

Linares

SANTA ANNA

Victoria

AMPUDIA

San Luis Potosí

Taken by Americans Nov. 1846

Tampico

SCOTT

Tuxpan

Campeche

M E X I C O

MEXICO CITY
see inset

Jalapa

Veracruz

Puebla

SCOTT

[Inset]

Guadalupe Hidalgo (Treaty of Guadalupe Hidalgo Feb. 2, 1848)

4

SANTA ANNA

MEXICO CITY

3

Tlaxcala

2

SCOTT

Popocatépetl

Puebla

1 CONTRERAS
2 CHURUBUSCO
3 MOLINA DEL REY
4 CHAPULTEPEC

Jalapa

CERRO GORDO

Gulf of Mexico

SANTA ANNA

Orizaba (Citlaltépetl)

Veracruz
Surrendered to Americans Mar. 29

Orizaba

Miles
0   20   40

© Copyright HAMMOND INCORPORATED, Maplewood, N.J.
Printed in U.S.A.

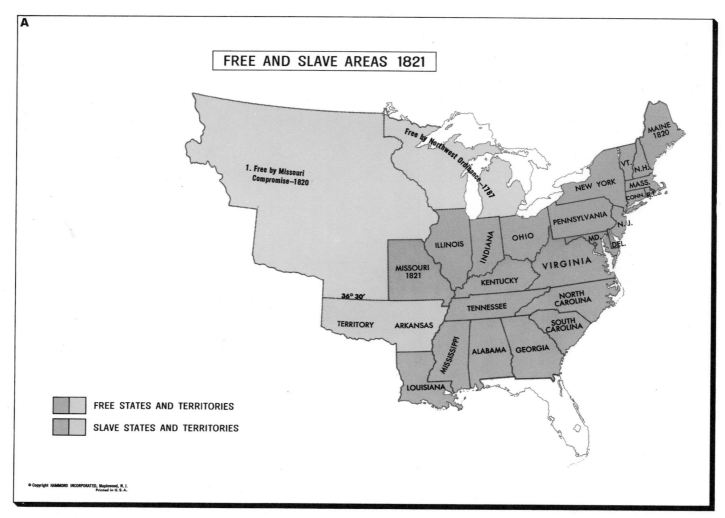

FREE AND SLAVE AREAS 1821

Free by Northwest Ordinance—1787

1. Free by Missouri Compromise—1820

MAINE 1820

VT. N.H.

NEW YORK

MASS.
CONN. R.I.

PENNSYLVANIA

N.J.

ILLINOIS INDIANA OHIO

MD. DEL.

MISSOURI 1821

VIRGINIA

KENTUCKY

36° 30'

NORTH CAROLINA

TENNESSEE

TERRITORY ARKANSAS

SOUTH CAROLINA

MISSISSIPPI ALABAMA GEORGIA

LOUISIANA

FREE STATES AND TERRITORIES

SLAVE STATES AND TERRITORIES

© Copyright HAMMOND INCORPORATED, Maplewood, N.J.
Printed in U.S.A.

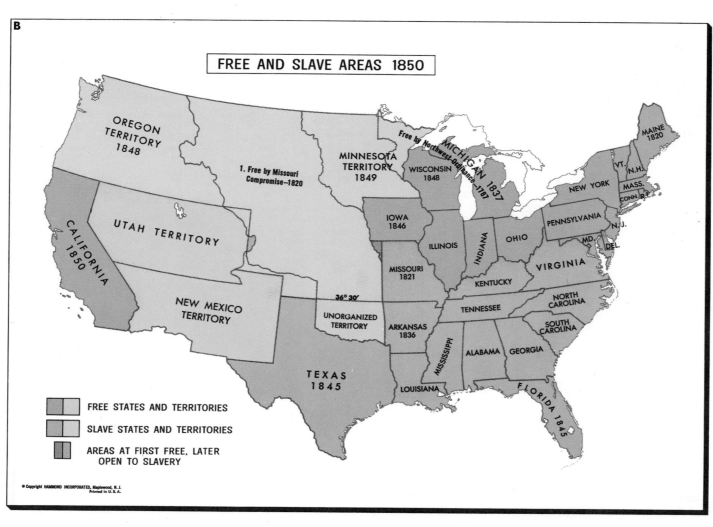

FREE AND SLAVE AREAS 1850

OREGON TERRITORY 1848

Free by Northwest Ordinance—1787

MICHIGAN 1837

MAINE 1820

1. Free by Missouri Compromise—1820

MINNESOTA TERRITORY 1849

WISCONSIN 1848

VT. N.H.

NEW YORK

MASS.
CONN. R.I.

UTAH TERRITORY

IOWA 1846

PENNSYLVANIA

N.J.

CALIFORNIA 1850

ILLINOIS INDIANA OHIO

MD. DEL.

MISSOURI 1821

VIRGINIA

NEW MEXICO TERRITORY

KENTUCKY

36° 30'

NORTH CAROLINA

UNORGANIZED TERRITORY

TENNESSEE

ARKANSAS 1836

SOUTH CAROLINA

MISSISSIPPI ALABAMA GEORGIA

TEXAS 1845

LOUISIANA

FLORIDA 1845

FREE STATES AND TERRITORIES

SLAVE STATES AND TERRITORIES

AREAS AT FIRST FREE, LATER OPEN TO SLAVERY

© Copyright HAMMOND INCORPORATED, Maplewood, N.J.
Printed in U.S.A.

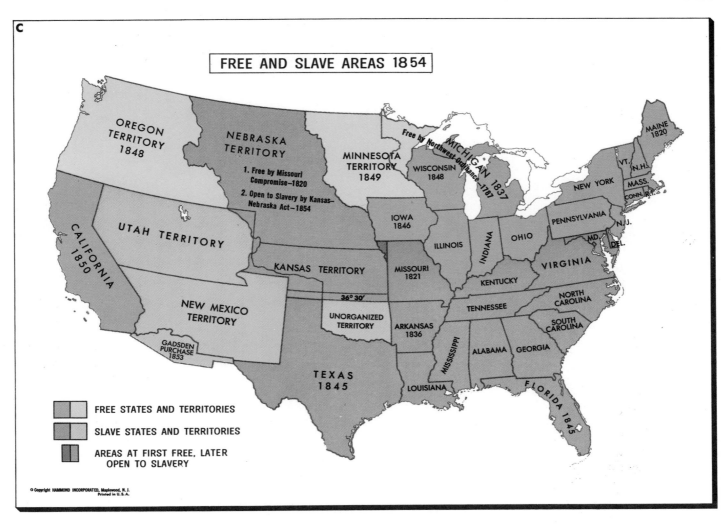

C

FREE AND SLAVE AREAS 1854

OREGON TERRITORY 1848

NEBRASKA TERRITORY

1. Free by Missouri Compromise–1820
2. Open to Slavery by Kansas–Nebraska Act–1854

MINNESOTA TERRITORY 1849

Free by Northwest Ordinance–1787

MICHIGAN 1837

WISCONSIN 1848

MAINE 1820

UTAH TERRITORY

CALIFORNIA 1850

IOWA 1846

NEW YORK

VT. N.H. MASS. CONN. R.I.

PENNSYLVANIA

N.J.

ILLINOIS INDIANA OHIO

MD. DEL.

KANSAS TERRITORY

MISSOURI 1821

VIRGINIA

NEW MEXICO TERRITORY

36° 30'

KENTUCKY

UNORGANIZED TERRITORY

TENNESSEE

NORTH CAROLINA

GADSDEN PURCHASE 1853

ARKANSAS 1836

SOUTH CAROLINA

MISSISSIPPI ALABAMA GEORGIA

TEXAS 1845

LOUISIANA

FLORIDA 1845

FREE STATES AND TERRITORIES

SLAVE STATES AND TERRITORIES

AREAS AT FIRST FREE, LATER OPEN TO SLAVERY

© Copyright HAMMOND INCORPORATED, Maplewood, N.J.
Printed in U.S.A.

D

FREE AND SLAVE AREAS 1861
at the outbreak of the Civil War

WASHINGTON TERRITORY

DAKOTA TERRITORY

OREGON 1859

MINNESOTA 1858

MICHIGAN

MAINE

NEVADA TERRITORY

UTAH TERRITORY

COLORADO TERRITORY

NEBRASKA TERRITORY

WISCONSIN

IOWA

NEW YORK

VT. N.H. MASS. CONN. R.I.

CALIFORNIA

KANSAS 1861

MISSOURI

PENNSYLVANIA

MASON-DIXON LINE

MD. DEL.

N.J.

ILLINOIS INDIANA OHIO

PUBLIC LAND

VIRGINIA

NEW MEXICO TERRITORY

INDIAN TERRITORY

ARKANSAS

KENTUCKY

TENNESSEE

NORTH CAROLINA

SOUTH CAROLINA

MISSISSIPPI ALABAMA GEORGIA

TEXAS

LOUISIANA

FLORIDA

FREE STATES

SLAVE STATES

TERRITORIES OPEN TO SLAVERY BY DRED SCOTT DECISION 1857

© Copyright HAMMOND INCORPORATED, Maplewood, N.J.
Printed in U.S.A.

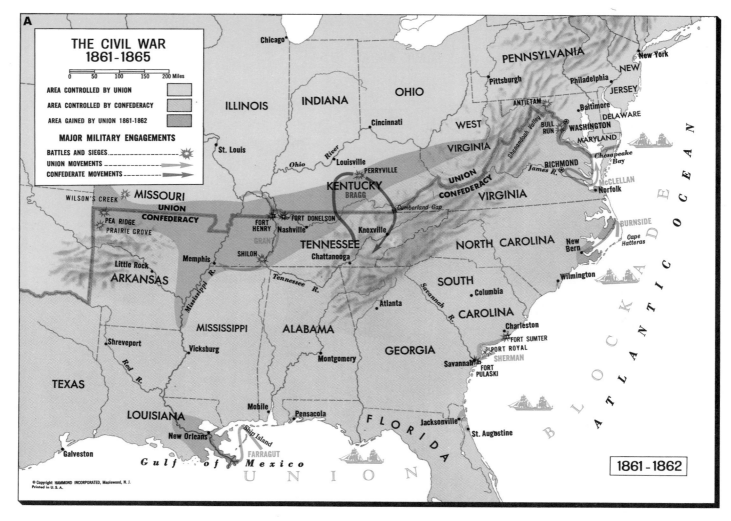

A

THE CIVIL WAR
1861-1865

0   50   100   150   200 Miles

AREA CONTROLLED BY UNION
AREA CONTROLLED BY CONFEDERACY
AREA GAINED BY UNION 1861-1862

MAJOR MILITARY ENGAGEMENTS

BATTLES AND SIEGES
UNION MOVEMENTS
CONFEDERATE MOVEMENTS

1861-1862

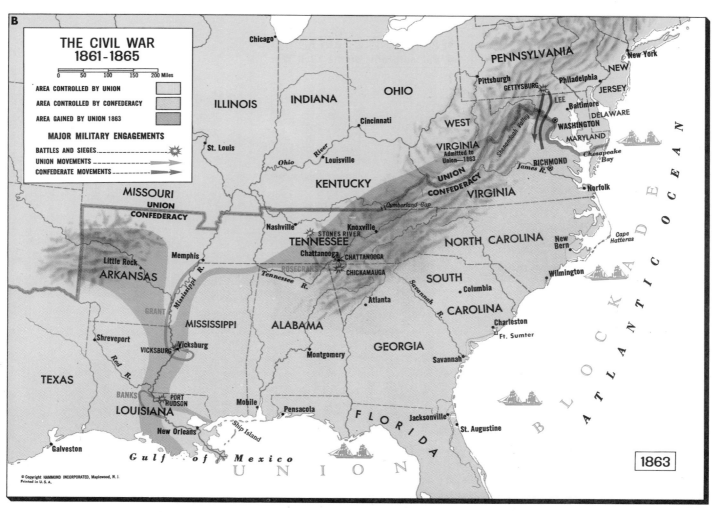

B

THE CIVIL WAR
1861-1865

0   50   100   150   200 Miles

AREA CONTROLLED BY UNION
AREA CONTROLLED BY CONFEDERACY
AREA GAINED BY UNION 1863

MAJOR MILITARY ENGAGEMENTS

BATTLES AND SIEGES
UNION MOVEMENTS
CONFEDERATE MOVEMENTS

1863

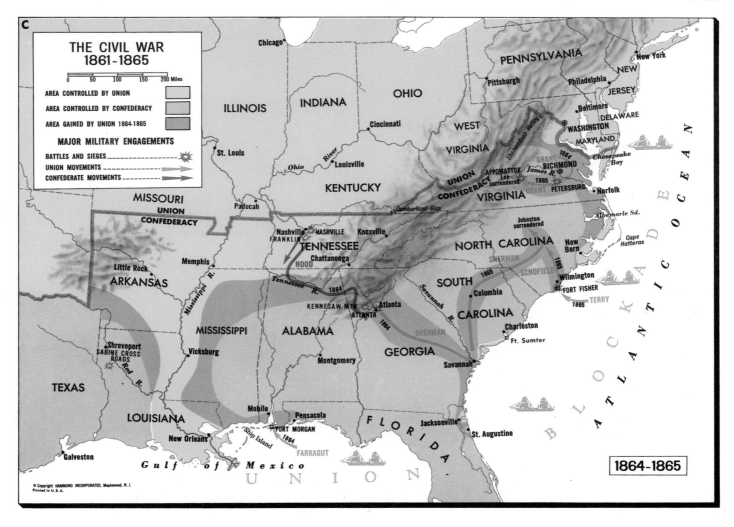

C

THE CIVIL WAR
1861-1865

0   50   100   150   200 Miles

AREA CONTROLLED BY UNION

AREA CONTROLLED BY CONFEDERACY

AREA GAINED BY UNION 1864-1865

MAJOR MILITARY ENGAGEMENTS

BATTLES AND SIEGES

UNION MOVEMENTS

CONFEDERATE MOVEMENTS

1864-1865

© Copyright HAMMOND INCORPORATED, Maplewood, N.J.
Printed in U.S.A.

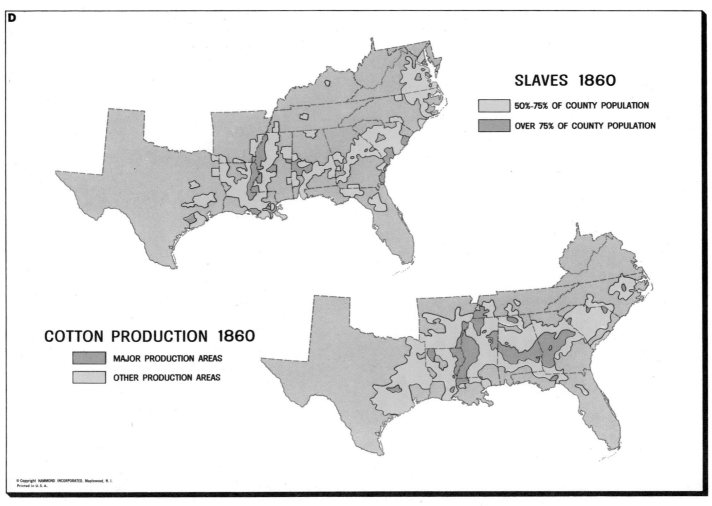

D

COTTON PRODUCTION 1860

MAJOR PRODUCTION AREAS

OTHER PRODUCTION AREAS

SLAVES 1860

50%-75% OF COUNTY POPULATION

OVER 75% OF COUNTY POPULATION

© Copyright HAMMOND INCORPORATED, Maplewood, N.J.
Printed in U.S.A.

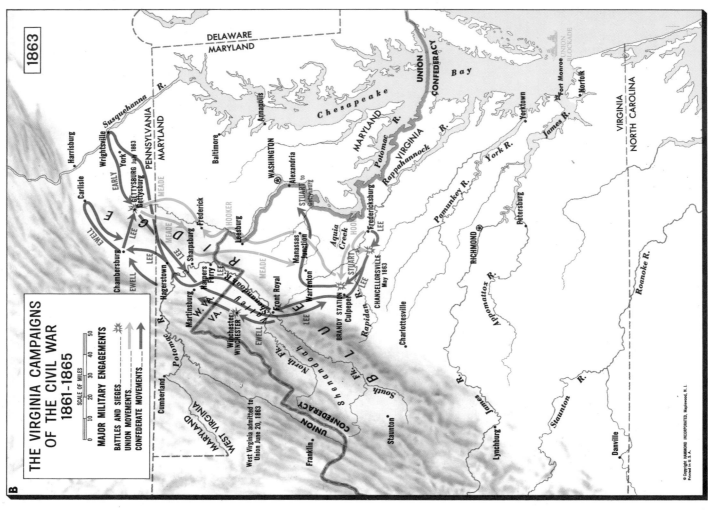

1863

THE VIRGINIA CAMPAIGNS OF THE CIVIL WAR 1861-1865

SCALE OF MILES

0 10 20 30 40 50

MAJOR MILITARY ENGAGEMENTS

BATTLES AND SIEGES

UNION MOVEMENTS

CONFEDERATE MOVEMENTS

West Virginia admitted to Union June 20, 1863

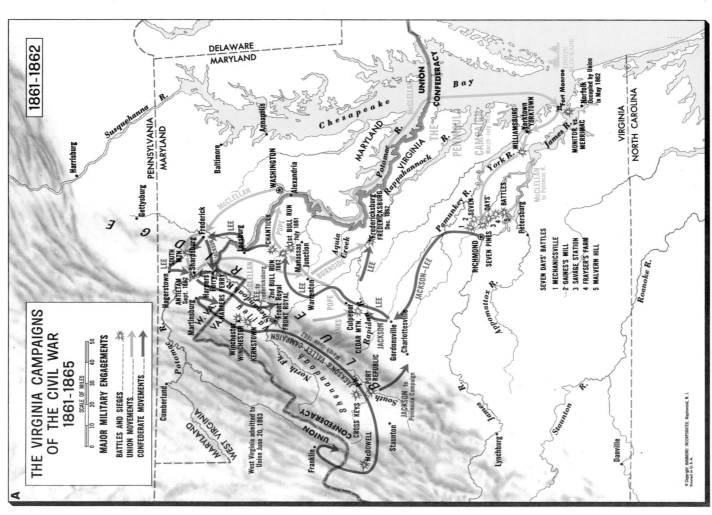

1861-1862

THE VIRGINIA CAMPAIGNS OF THE CIVIL WAR 1861-1865

SCALE OF MILES

0 10 20 30 40 50

MAJOR MILITARY ENGAGEMENTS

BATTLES AND SIEGES

UNION MOVEMENTS

CONFEDERATE MOVEMENTS

West Virginia admitted to Union June 20, 1863

SEVEN DAYS' BATTLES
1 MECHANICSVILLE
2 GAINES'S MILL
3 SAVAGE STATION
4 FRAYSER'S FARM
5 MALVERN HILL

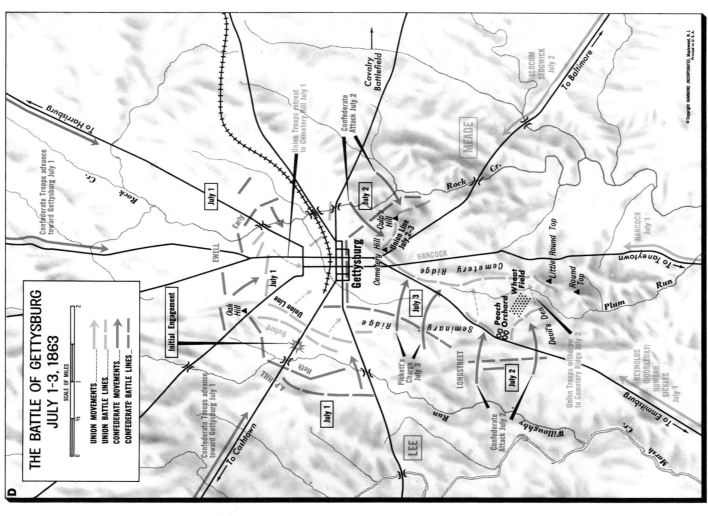

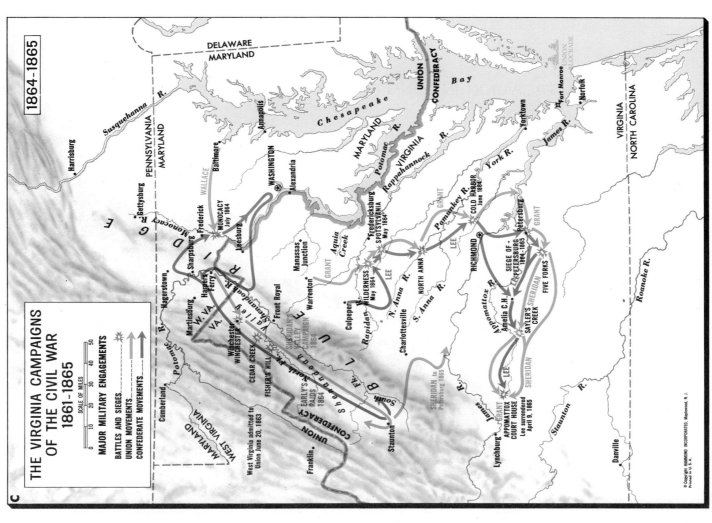

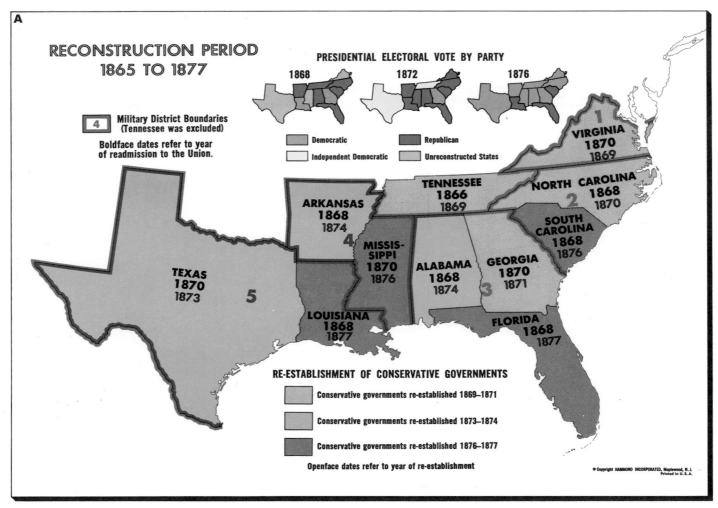

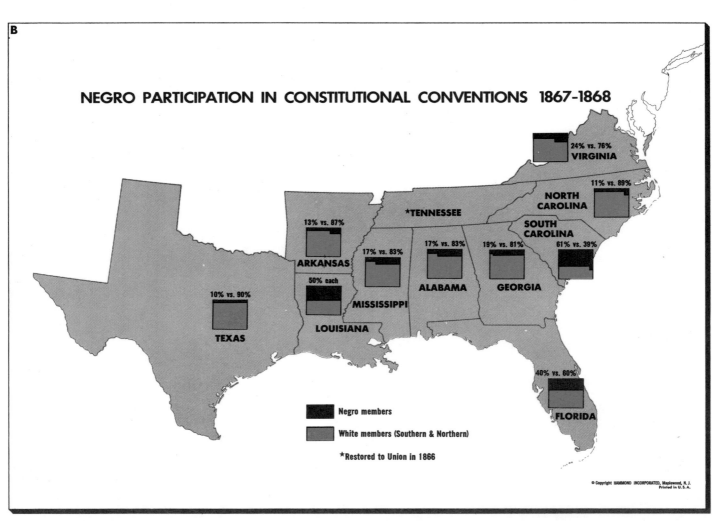

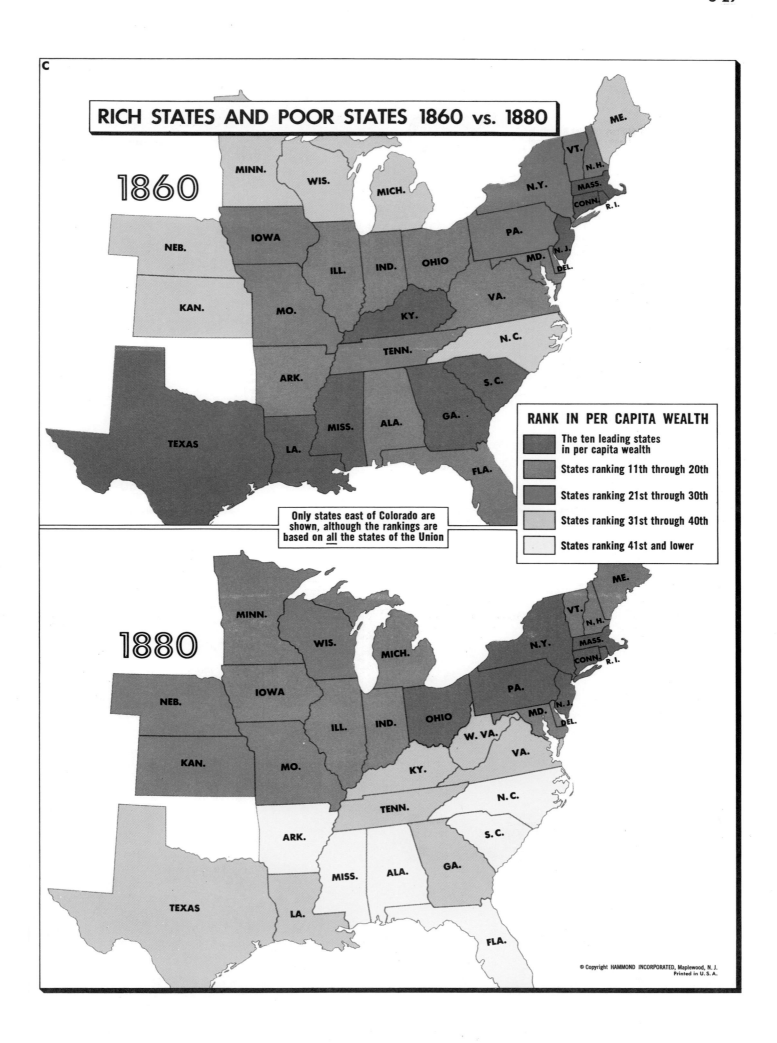

RICH STATES AND POOR STATES 1860 vs. 1880

1860

1880

Only states east of Colorado are shown, although the rankings are based on all the states of the Union

RANK IN PER CAPITA WEALTH

- The ten leading states in per capita wealth
- States ranking 11th through 20th
- States ranking 21st through 30th
- States ranking 31st through 40th
- States ranking 41st and lower

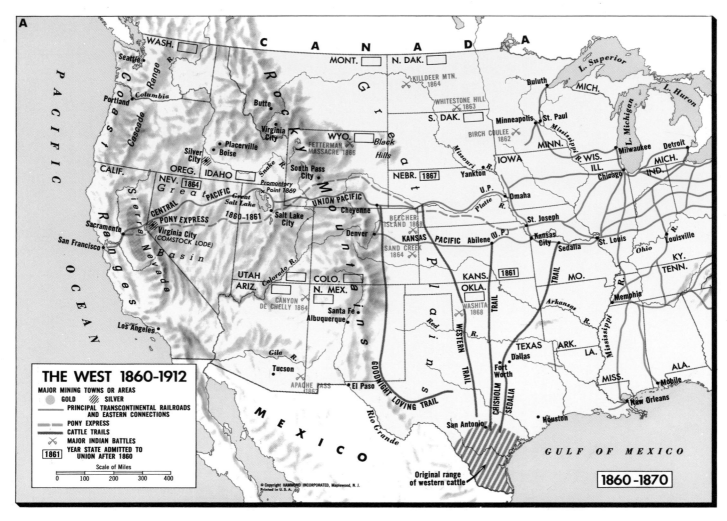

A

THE WEST 1860-1912

MAJOR MINING TOWNS OR AREAS
- GOLD
- SILVER

— PRINCIPAL TRANSCONTINENTAL RAILROADS AND EASTERN CONNECTIONS
— PONY EXPRESS
— CATTLE TRAILS
✕ MAJOR INDIAN BATTLES

[1861] YEAR STATE ADMITTED TO UNION AFTER 1860

Scale of Miles
0 100 200 300 400

© Copyright HAMMOND INCORPORATED, Maplewood, N.J.
Printed in U.S.A.

1860-1870

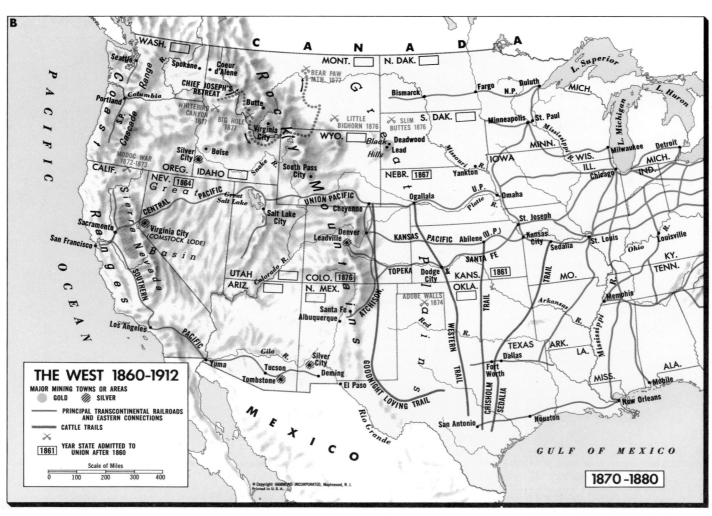

B

THE WEST 1860-1912

MAJOR MINING TOWNS OR AREAS
- GOLD
- SILVER

— PRINCIPAL TRANSCONTINENTAL RAILROADS AND EASTERN CONNECTIONS
— CATTLE TRAILS
✕

[1861] YEAR STATE ADMITTED TO UNION AFTER 1860

Scale of Miles
0 100 200 300 400

© Copyright HAMMOND INCORPORATED, Maplewood, N.J.
Printed in U.S.A.

1870-1880

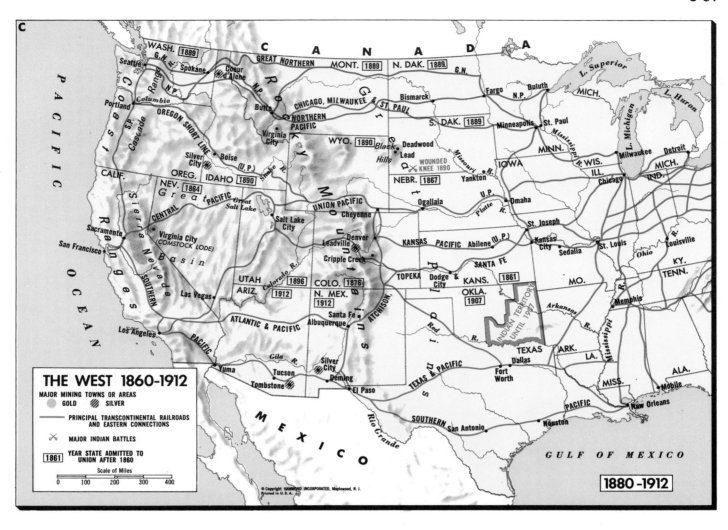

THE WEST 1860-1912

MAJOR MINING TOWNS OR AREAS
- ● GOLD
- ◢ SILVER

—— PRINCIPAL TRANSCONTINENTAL RAILROADS AND EASTERN CONNECTIONS

✕ MAJOR INDIAN BATTLES

[1861] YEAR STATE ADMITTED TO UNION AFTER 1860

Scale of Miles
0 100 200 300 400

© Copyright HAMMOND INCORPORATED, Maplewood, N.J.
Printed in U.S.A.

[1880-1912]

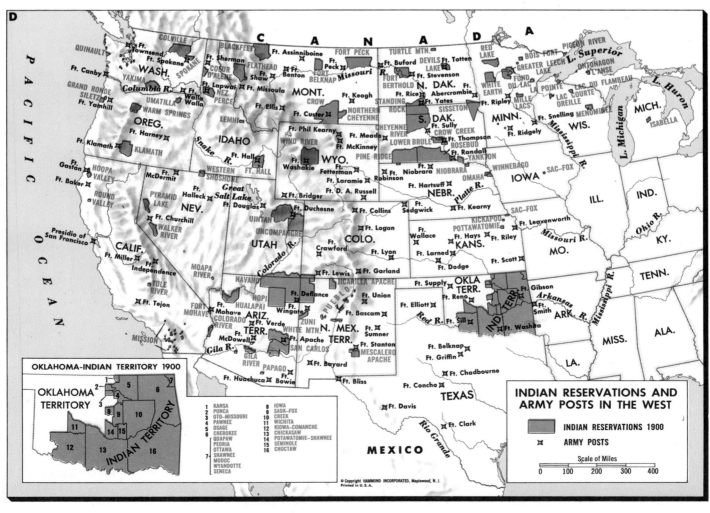

OKLAHOMA-INDIAN TERRITORY 1900

OKLAHOMA TERRITORY
INDIAN TERRITORY

1 KANSA
2 PONCA
3 OTO-MISSOURI
4 PAWNEE
5 OSAGE
6 CHEROKEE
7 QUAPAW
  PEORIA
  OTTAWA
  SHAWNEE
  MODOC
  WYANDOTTE
  SENECA
8 SAUK-FOX
9 CREEK
10 IOWA
11 WICHITA
12 KIOWA-COMANCHE
13 CHICKASAW
14 POTAWATOMIE-SHAWNEE
15 SEMINOLE
16 CHOCTAW

INDIAN RESERVATIONS AND ARMY POSTS IN THE WEST

▨ INDIAN RESERVATIONS 1900
✕ ARMY POSTS

Scale of Miles
0 100 200 300 400

© Copyright HAMMOND INCORPORATED, Maplewood, N.J.
Printed in U.S.A.

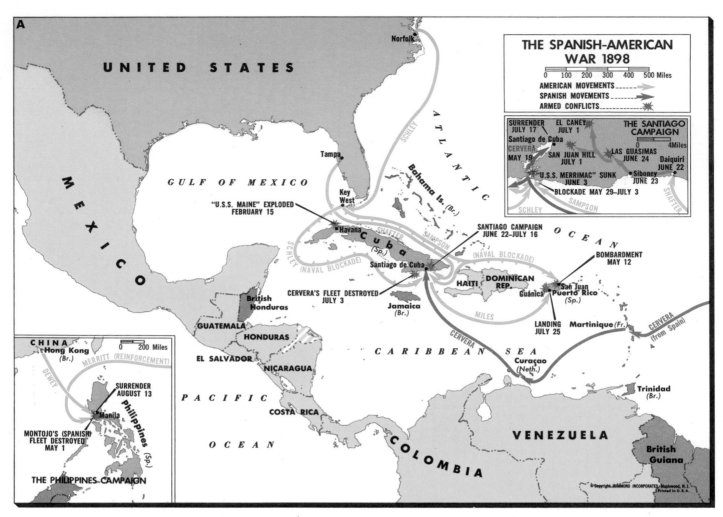

A

UNITED STATES

THE SPANISH-AMERICAN
WAR 1898

0   100   200   300   400   500 Miles

AMERICAN MOVEMENTS
SPANISH MOVEMENTS
ARMED CONFLICTS

THE SANTIAGO
CAMPAIGN

SURRENDER   EL CANEY
JULY 17   JULY 1
Santiago de Cuba
CERVERA   LAS GUASIMAS
MAY 19   SAN JUAN HILL   JUNE 24
          JULY 1   Daiquiri
          "U.S.S. MERRIMAC" SUNK   Siboney JUNE 22
          JUNE 3   JUNE 23
          BLOCKADE MAY 29–JULY 3

0   4 Miles

MEXICO

GULF OF MEXICO

Norfolk

Tampa

Key West

"U.S.S. MAINE" EXPLODED
FEBRUARY 15

SHAFTER

Havana
Cuba
(Sp.)

Santiago de Cuba

CERVERA'S FLEET DESTROYED
JULY 3

Bahama Is.
(Br.)

ATLANTIC   OCEAN

SANTIAGO CAMPAIGN
JUNE 22–JULY 16

(NAVAL BLOCKADE)

SCHLEY (NAVAL BLOCKADE)

HAITI   DOMINICAN
REP.

BOMBARDMENT
MAY 12

San Juan
Guánica   Puerto Rico
(Sp.)

Jamaica
(Br.)

MILES

LANDING
JULY 25   Martinique (Fr.)

CERVERA
(from Spain)

British
Honduras

GUATEMALA

HONDURAS

EL SALVADOR

NICARAGUA

COSTA RICA

CARIBBEAN   SEA

Curaçao
(Neth.)

Trinidad
(Br.)

CHINA
Hong Kong
(Br.)

0   200 Miles

MERRITT (REINFORCEMENT)

DEWEY

SURRENDER
AUGUST 13

Manila

Philippines (Sp.)

MONTOJO'S (SPANISH)
FLEET DESTROYED
MAY 1

THE PHILIPPINES CAMPAIGN

PACIFIC

OCEAN

VENEZUELA

COLOMBIA

British
Guiana

© Copyright HAMMOND INCORPORATED, Maplewood, N.J.
Printed in U.S.A.

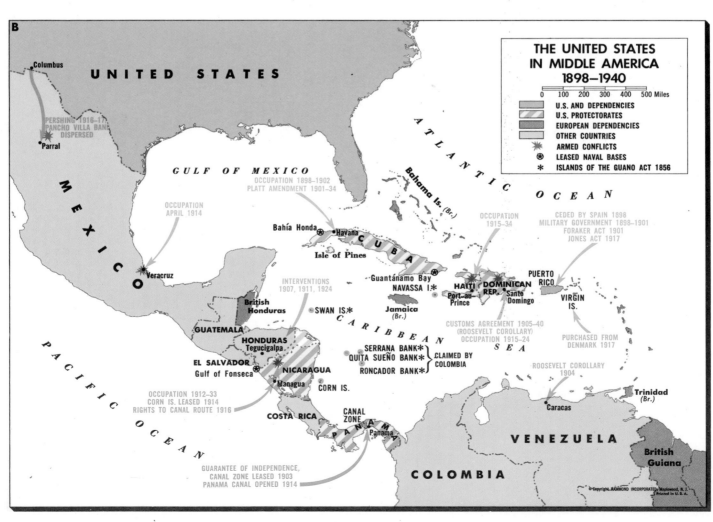

B

Columbus

UNITED STATES

THE UNITED STATES
IN MIDDLE AMERICA
1898–1940

0   100   200   300   400   500 Miles

U.S. AND DEPENDENCIES
U.S. PROTECTORATES
EUROPEAN DEPENDENCIES
OTHER COUNTRIES
ARMED CONFLICTS
LEASED NAVAL BASES
ISLANDS OF THE GUANO ACT 1856

PERSHING 1916–17
PANCHO VILLA BAND
DISPERSED

Parral

MEXICO

GULF OF MEXICO

OCCUPATION 1898–1902
PLATT AMENDMENT 1901–34

OCCUPATION
APRIL 1914

Veracruz

Bahía Honda

Havana
CUBA

Isle of Pines

Bahama Is.
(Br.)

ATLANTIC   OCEAN

OCCUPATION
1915–34

CEDED BY SPAIN 1898
MILITARY GOVERNMENT 1898–1901
FORAKER ACT 1901
JONES ACT 1917

INTERVENTIONS
1907, 1911, 1924

Guantánamo Bay
NAVASSA I.

Jamaica
(Br.)

Guantánamo Bay

HAITI   DOMINICAN
Port-au- REP.
Prince   Santo
         Domingo

PUERTO
RICO

VIRGIN
IS.

British
Honduras

SWAN IS.

CARIBBEAN

CUSTOMS AGREEMENT 1905–40
(ROOSEVELT COROLLARY)
OCCUPATION 1915–24

PURCHASED FROM
DENMARK 1917

GUATEMALA

HONDURAS
Tegucigalpa

EL SALVADOR
Gulf of Fonseca

SERRANA BANK
QUITA SUEÑO BANK   CLAIMED BY
RONCADOR BANK   COLOMBIA

SEA

ROOSEVELT COROLLARY
1904

NICARAGUA
Managua

CORN IS.

OCCUPATION 1912–33
CORN IS. LEASED 1914
RIGHTS TO CANAL ROUTE 1916

COSTA RICA

CANAL
ZONE
Panama

PANAMA

Trinidad
(Br.)

Caracas

PACIFIC   OCEAN

GUARANTEE OF INDEPENDENCE,
CANAL ZONE LEASED 1903
PANAMA CANAL OPENED 1914

VENEZUELA

COLOMBIA

British
Guiana

© Copyright HAMMOND INCORPORATED, Maplewood, N.J.
Printed in U.S.A.

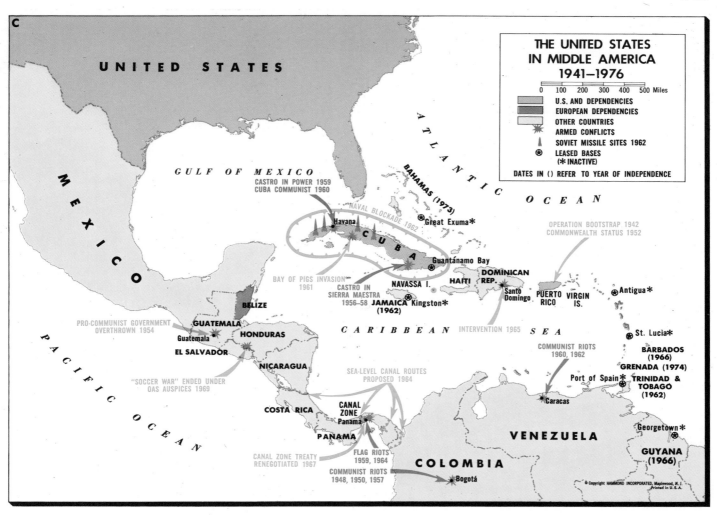

THE UNITED STATES IN MIDDLE AMERICA 1941–1976

0 100 200 300 400 500 Miles

U.S. AND DEPENDENCIES
EUROPEAN DEPENDENCIES
OTHER COUNTRIES
ARMED CONFLICTS
SOVIET MISSILE SITES 1962
LEASED BASES (* INACTIVE)

DATES IN ( ) REFER TO YEAR OF INDEPENDENCE

UNITED STATES

GULF OF MEXICO

MEXICO

ATLANTIC OCEAN

BAHAMAS (1973)

CASTRO IN POWER 1959
CUBA COMMUNIST 1960

NAVAL BLOCKADE 1962

Great Exuma*

Havana

CUBA

Guantánamo Bay

OPERATION BOOTSTRAP 1942
COMMONWEALTH STATUS 1952

BAY OF PIGS INVASION 1961

CASTRO IN SIERRA MAESTRA 1956–58

NAVASSA I.

HAITI

DOMINICAN REP.

Santo Domingo

PUERTO RICO

VIRGIN IS.

Antigua*

JAMAICA (1962) Kingston*

PRO-COMMUNIST GOVERNMENT OVERTHROWN 1954

BELIZE

GUATEMALA

Guatemala

HONDURAS

EL SALVADOR

NICARAGUA

CARIBBEAN   INTERVENTION 1965   SEA

St. Lucia*

COMMUNIST RIOTS 1960, 1962

BARBADOS (1966)
GRENADA (1974)

Port of Spain*

TRINIDAD & TOBAGO (1962)

"SOCCER WAR" ENDED UNDER OAS AUSPICES 1969

SEA-LEVEL CANAL ROUTES PROPOSED 1964

COSTA RICA

CANAL ZONE
Panama

PANAMA

Caracas

VENEZUELA

Georgetown*

GUYANA (1966)

CANAL ZONE TREATY RENEGOTIATED 1967

FLAG RIOTS 1959, 1964

COMMUNIST RIOTS 1948, 1950, 1957

COLOMBIA

Bogotá

PACIFIC OCEAN

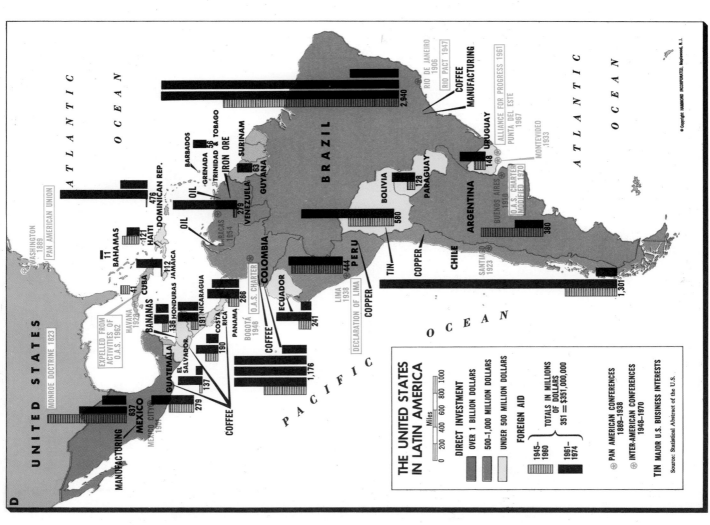

THE UNITED STATES IN LATIN AMERICA

Miles
0 200 400 600 800 1000

DIRECT INVESTMENT
OVER 1 BILLION DOLLARS
500–1,000 MILLION DOLLARS
UNDER 500 MILLION DOLLARS

FOREIGN AID
TOTALS IN MILLIONS OF DOLLARS
351 = $351,000,000,000
1945–1960
1961–1974

PAN AMERICAN CONFERENCES 1889–1938
INTER-AMERICAN CONFERENCES 1948–1970

TIN MAJOR U.S. BUSINESS INTERESTS

UNITED STATES

MANUFACTURING

MONROE DOCTRINE 1823

Washington 1889
PAN AMERICAN UNION

EXPELLED FROM ACTIVITIES OF O.A.S. 1962

Havana 1928

BAHAMAS
11

HAITI
121

476 DOMINICAN REP.

BARBADOS

GRENADA 56
TRINIDAD & TOBAGO

SURINAM

IRON ORE 83

GUYANA

COFFEE
MANUFACTURING

RIO DE JANEIRO 1906
RIO PACT 1947

2,940

ALLIANCE FOR PROGRESS 1961
PUNTA DEL ESTE 1967

MONTEVIDEO 1933

URUGUAY
148

CUBA
41

BANANAS

HONDURAS

NICARAGUA

112 JAMAICA

OIL

OIL
279 VENEZUELA

CARACAS 1954

COLOMBIA

286 O.A.S. CHARTER

BOGOTÁ 1948

ECUADOR

COFFEE
241

O.A.S. CHARTER

BRAZIL

PERU
444

LIMA 1938

DECLARATION OF LIMA

COFFEE

COPPER

BOLIVIA
580

PARAGUAY
128

O.A.S. CHARTER MODIFIED 1970

ARGENTINA
380

BUENOS AIRES 1910

CHILE

COPPER

SANTIAGO 1923

TIN

COPPER

1,301

MEXICO
637

MEXICO CITY 1951

GUATEMALA
279

EL SALVADOR
137

COSTA RICA
190

COFFEE

PANAMA

1,176

COFFEE

PACIFIC OCEAN

ATLANTIC OCEAN

ATLANTIC OCEAN

A

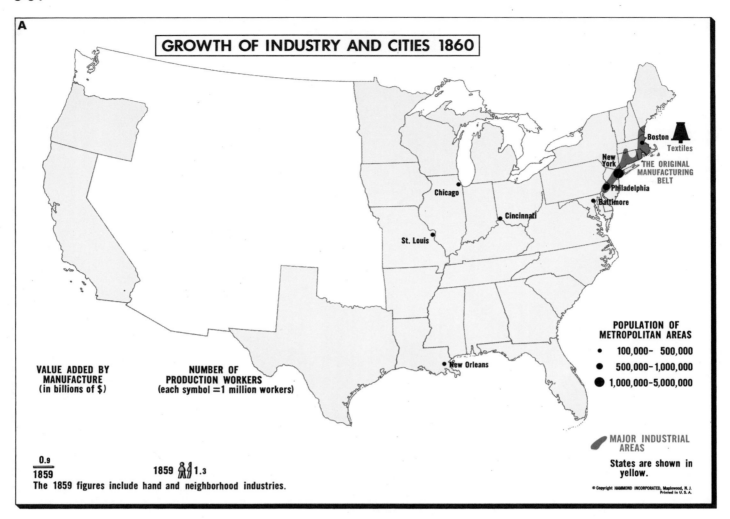

GROWTH OF INDUSTRY AND CITIES 1860

Boston
Textiles
New York
THE ORIGINAL MANUFACTURING BELT
Philadelphia
Baltimore
Chicago
Cincinnati
St. Louis
New Orleans

POPULATION OF METROPOLITAN AREAS

- · 100,000– 500,000
- ● 500,000–1,000,000
- ⬤ 1,000,000–5,000,000

VALUE ADDED BY MANUFACTURE (in billions of $)

NUMBER OF PRODUCTION WORKERS (each symbol =1 million workers)

MAJOR INDUSTRIAL AREAS

States are shown in yellow.

0.9
———
1859

1859 🧍🧍 1.3

The 1859 figures include hand and neighborhood industries.

© Copyright HAMMOND INCORPORATED, Maplewood, N.J.
Printed in U.S.A.

B

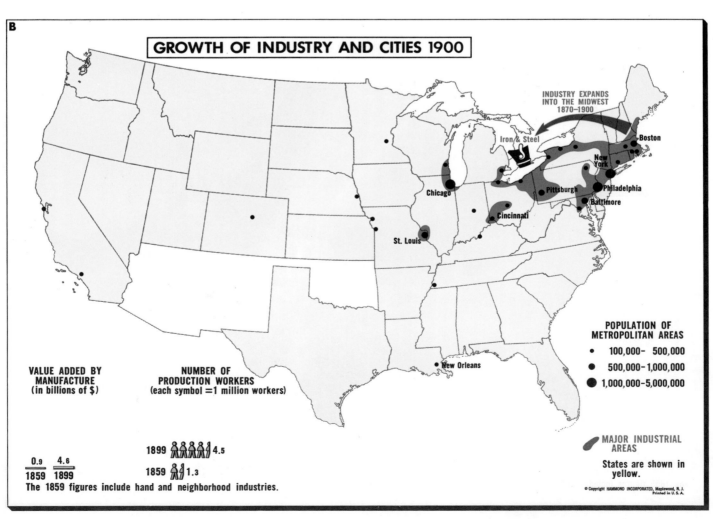

GROWTH OF INDUSTRY AND CITIES 1900

INDUSTRY EXPANDS INTO THE MIDWEST 1870–1900
Iron & Steel
Boston
New York
Chicago
Pittsburgh
Philadelphia
Baltimore
Cincinnati
St. Louis
New Orleans

POPULATION OF METROPOLITAN AREAS

- · 100,000– 500,000
- ● 500,000–1,000,000
- ⬤ 1,000,000–5,000,000

VALUE ADDED BY MANUFACTURE (in billions of $)

NUMBER OF PRODUCTION WORKERS (each symbol =1 million workers)

MAJOR INDUSTRIAL AREAS

States are shown in yellow.

1899 🧍🧍🧍🧍 4.5

0.9   4.6
——— ———
1859   1899

1859 🧍🧍 1.3

The 1859 figures include hand and neighborhood industries.

© Copyright HAMMOND INCORPORATED, Maplewood, N.J.
Printed in U.S.A.

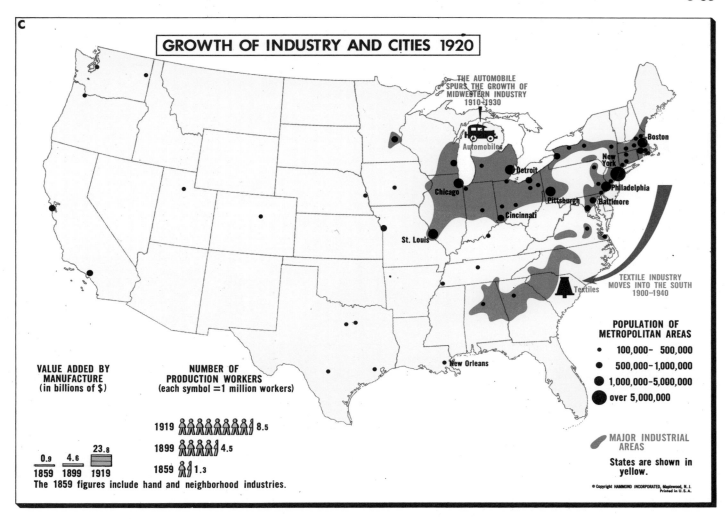

C

GROWTH OF INDUSTRY AND CITIES 1920

THE AUTOMOBILE
SPURS THE GROWTH OF
MIDWESTERN INDUSTRY
1910-1930

Automobiles

Boston
New York
Detroit
Philadelphia
Chicago
Pittsburgh
Baltimore
Cincinnati
St. Louis

TEXTILE INDUSTRY
MOVES INTO THE SOUTH
1900-1940

Textiles

New Orleans

**POPULATION OF
METROPOLITAN AREAS**

- 100,000- 500,000
- 500,000-1,000,000
- 1,000,000-5,000,000
- over 5,000,000

**VALUE ADDED BY
MANUFACTURE**
(in billions of $)

**NUMBER OF
PRODUCTION WORKERS**
(each symbol =1 million workers)

1919 8.5
1899 4.5
1859 1.3

0.9   4.6   23.8
1859 1899 1919

The 1859 figures include hand and neighborhood industries.

MAJOR INDUSTRIAL
AREAS

States are shown in
yellow.

© Copyright HAMMOND INCORPORATED, Maplewood, N. J.
Printed in U.S.A.

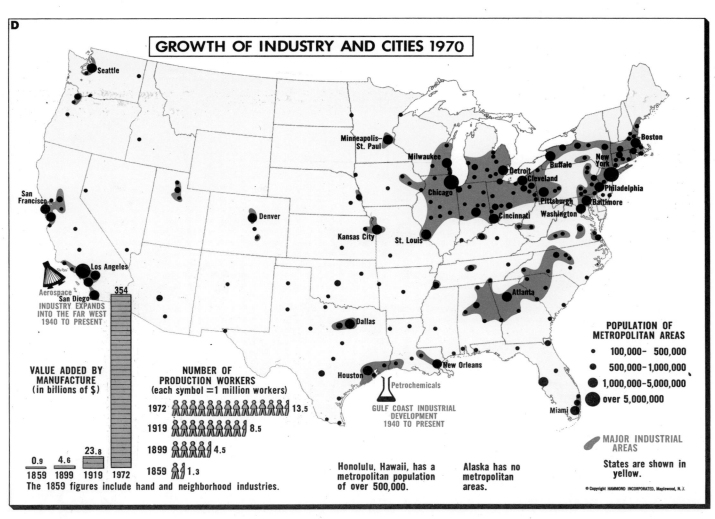

D

GROWTH OF INDUSTRY AND CITIES 1970

Seattle

Minneapolis-
St. Paul

Milwaukee

Buffalo
Detroit   New York
Cleveland
San
Francisco

Denver

Chicago
Pittsburgh   Philadelphia
Cincinnati   Baltimore
Kansas City   Washington
St. Louis

Los Angeles

Aerospace
San Diego
INDUSTRY EXPANDS
INTO THE FAR WEST
1940 TO PRESENT

354

Atlanta

Dallas

Houston

New Orleans

Petrochemicals
GULF COAST INDUSTRIAL
DEVELOPMENT
1940 TO PRESENT

Miami

**POPULATION OF
METROPOLITAN AREAS**

- 100,000- 500,000
- 500,000-1,000,000
- 1,000,000-5,000,000
- over 5,000,000

**VALUE ADDED BY
MANUFACTURE**
(in billions of $)

**NUMBER OF
PRODUCTION WORKERS**
(each symbol =1 million workers)

1972 13.5
1919 8.5
1899 4.5

0.9   4.6   23.8
1859 1899 1919 1972

1859 1.3

The 1859 figures include hand and neighborhood industries.

Honolulu, Hawaii, has a
metropolitan population
of over 500,000.

Alaska has no
metropolitan
areas.

MAJOR INDUSTRIAL
AREAS

States are shown in
yellow.

© Copyright HAMMOND INCORPORATED, Maplewood, N. J.

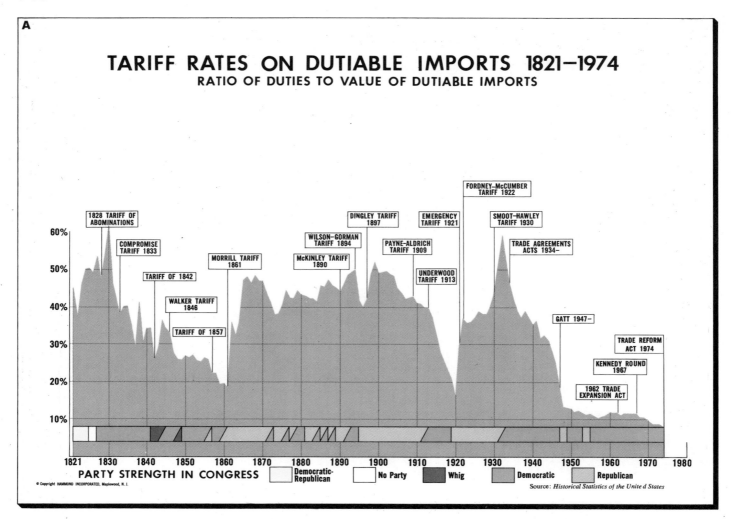

A

TARIFF RATES ON DUTIABLE IMPORTS 1821–1974
RATIO OF DUTIES TO VALUE OF DUTIABLE IMPORTS

FORDNEY–McCUMBER TARIFF 1922

1828 TARIFF OF ABOMINATIONS

COMPROMISE TARIFF 1833

DINGLEY TARIFF 1897

EMERGENCY TARIFF 1921

SMOOT–HAWLEY TARIFF 1930

WILSON–GORMAN TARIFF 1894

TARIFF OF 1842

PAYNE–ALDRICH TARIFF 1909

TRADE AGREEMENTS ACTS 1934–

MORRILL TARIFF 1861

McKINLEY TARIFF 1890

WALKER TARIFF 1846

UNDERWOOD TARIFF 1913

TARIFF OF 1857

GATT 1947–

TRADE REFORM ACT 1974

KENNEDY ROUND 1967

1962 TRADE EXPANSION ACT

60%
50%
40%
30%
20%
10%

1821 1830 1840 1850 1860 1870 1880 1890 1900 1910 1920 1930 1940 1950 1960 1970 1980

PARTY STRENGTH IN CONGRESS
Democratic-Republican   No Party   Whig   Democratic   Republican

© Copyright HAMMOND INCORPORATED, Maplewood, N.J.

Source: *Historical Statistics of the United States*

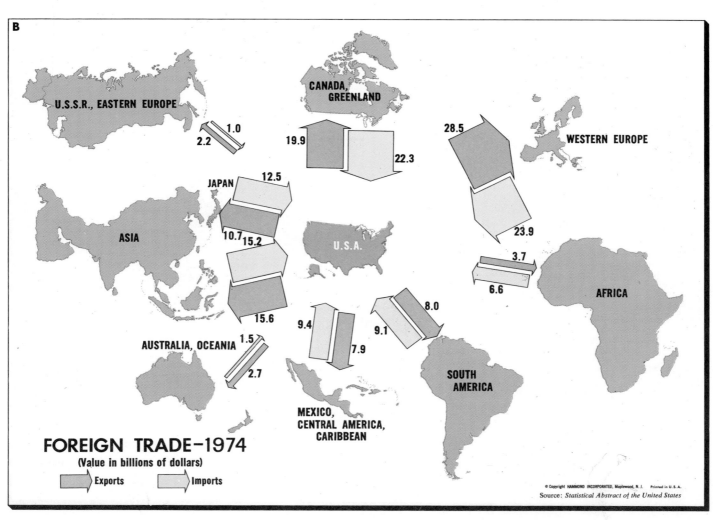

B

U.S.S.R., EASTERN EUROPE

CANADA, GREENLAND

WESTERN EUROPE

1.0
2.2

19.9   22.3

28.5

JAPAN   12.5

23.9

ASIA

10.7 15.2

U.S.A.

3.7
6.6

AFRICA

15.6

8.0

9.4   9.1

AUSTRALIA, OCEANIA   1.5

7.9

2.7

SOUTH AMERICA

MEXICO, CENTRAL AMERICA, CARIBBEAN

FOREIGN TRADE–1974
(Value in billions of dollars)

Exports   Imports

© Copyright HAMMOND INCORPORATED, Maplewood, N.J.   Printed in U.S.A.

Source: *Statistical Abstract of the United States*

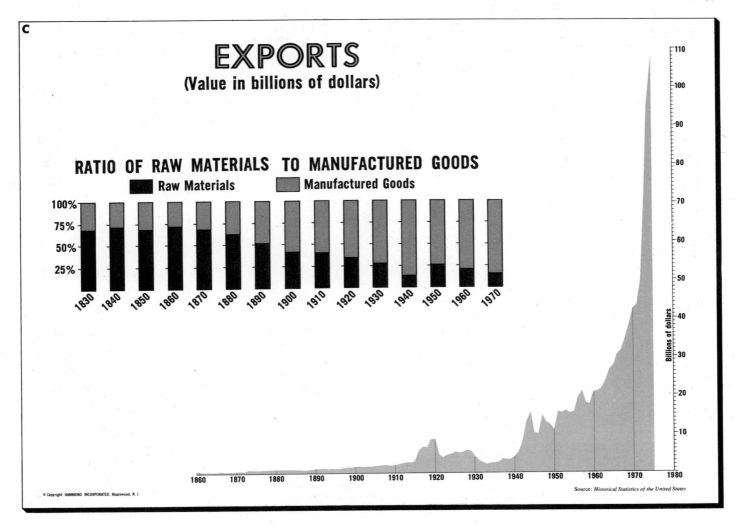

EXPORTS
(Value in billions of dollars)

C

RATIO OF RAW MATERIALS TO MANUFACTURED GOODS
■ Raw Materials ▨ Manufactured Goods

1830 1840 1850 1860 1870 1880 1890 1900 1910 1920 1930 1940 1950 1960 1970

© Copyright HAMMOND INCORPORATED, Maplewood, N.J.

Source: *Historical Statistics of the United States*

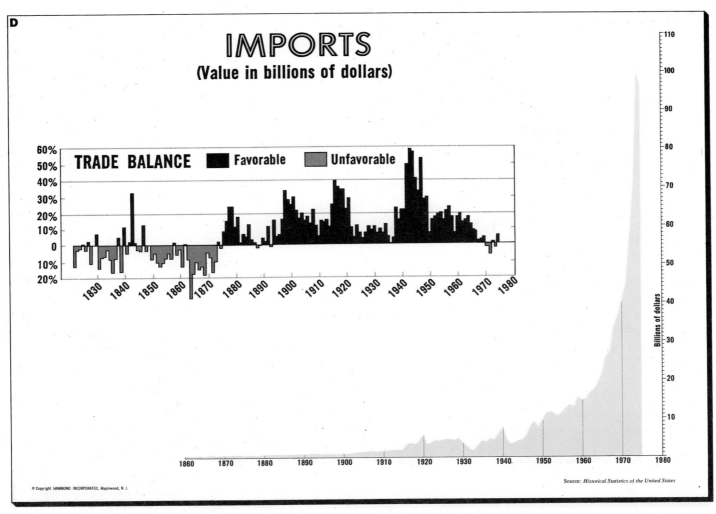

IMPORTS
(Value in billions of dollars)

D

TRADE BALANCE ■ Favorable ▨ Unfavorable

© Copyright HAMMOND INCORPORATED, Maplewood, N.J.

Source: *Historical Statistics of the United States*

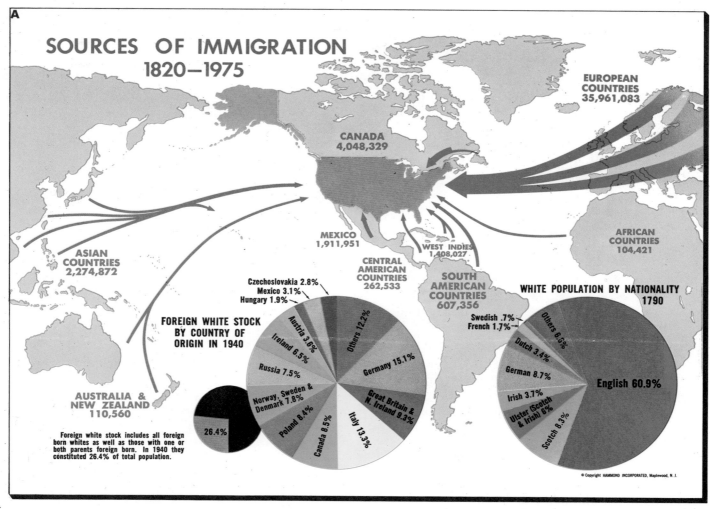

A

SOURCES OF IMMIGRATION
1820–1975

EUROPEAN
COUNTRIES
35,961,083

CANADA
4,048,329

ASIAN
COUNTRIES
2,274,872

AUSTRALIA &
NEW ZEALAND
110,560

MEXICO
1,911,951

WEST INDIES
1,408,027

CENTRAL
AMERICAN
COUNTRIES
262,533

SOUTH
AMERICAN
COUNTRIES
607,356

AFRICAN
COUNTRIES
104,421

**FOREIGN WHITE STOCK
BY COUNTRY OF
ORIGIN IN 1940**

Czechoslovakia 2.8%
Mexico 3.1%
Hungary 1.9%
Austria 3.6%
Ireland 6.5%
Russia 7.5%
Others 12.2%
Germany 15.1%
Norway, Sweden &
Denmark 7.8%
Great Britain &
N. Ireland 9.3%
Poland 8.4%
Canada 8.5%
Italy 13.3%

26.4%

Foreign white stock includes all foreign
born whites as well as those with one or
both parents foreign born. In 1940 they
constituted 26.4% of total population.

**WHITE POPULATION BY NATIONALITY
1790**

Swedish .7%
French 1.7%
Others 6.6%
Dutch 3.4%
German 8.7%
Irish 3.7%
Ulster (Scotch
& Irish) 6%
Scotch 8.3%
English 60.9%

© Copyright HAMMOND INCORPORATED, Maplewood, N. J.

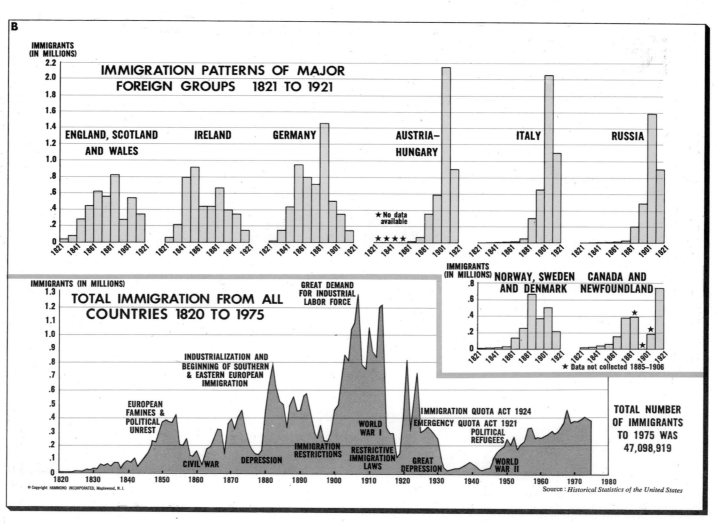

B

IMMIGRANTS
(IN MILLIONS)

IMMIGRATION PATTERNS OF MAJOR
FOREIGN GROUPS   1821 TO 1921

**ENGLAND, SCOTLAND
AND WALES**

IRELAND

GERMANY

**AUSTRIA–
HUNGARY**

★ No data
available

ITALY

RUSSIA

IMMIGRANTS (IN MILLIONS)

TOTAL IMMIGRATION FROM ALL
COUNTRIES 1820 TO 1975

GREAT DEMAND
FOR INDUSTRIAL
LABOR FORCE

INDUSTRIALIZATION AND
BEGINNING OF SOUTHERN
& EASTERN EUROPEAN
IMMIGRATION

EUROPEAN
FAMINES &
POLITICAL
UNREST

CIVIL WAR

DEPRESSION

IMMIGRATION
RESTRICTIONS

WORLD
WAR I

RESTRICTIVE
IMMIGRATION
LAWS

IMMIGRATION QUOTA ACT 1924
EMERGENCY QUOTA ACT 1921
POLITICAL
REFUGEES

GREAT
DEPRESSION

WORLD
WAR II

IMMIGRANTS
(IN MILLIONS)

**NORWAY, SWEDEN
AND DENMARK**

**CANADA AND
NEWFOUNDLAND**

★ Data not collected 1885–1906

**TOTAL NUMBER
OF IMMIGRANTS
TO 1975 WAS
47,098,919**

© Copyright HAMMOND INCORPORATED, Maplewood, N. J.

Source: *Historical Statistics of the United States*

DISTRIBUTION OF FOREIGN BORN IN UNITED STATES
1910

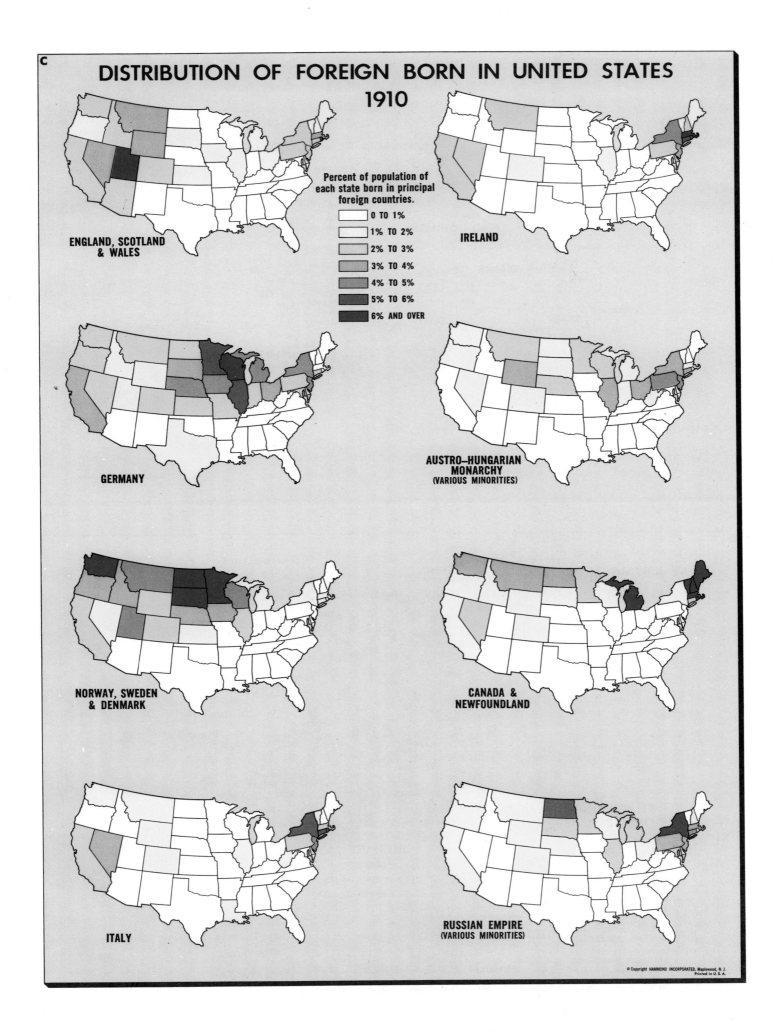

Percent of population of each state born in principal foreign countries.

- 0 TO 1%
- 1% TO 2%
- 2% TO 3%
- 3% TO 4%
- 4% TO 5%
- 5% TO 6%
- 6% AND OVER

ENGLAND, SCOTLAND & WALES

IRELAND

GERMANY

AUSTRO–HUNGARIAN MONARCHY
(VARIOUS MINORITIES)

NORWAY, SWEDEN & DENMARK

CANADA & NEWFOUNDLAND

ITALY

RUSSIAN EMPIRE
(VARIOUS MINORITIES)

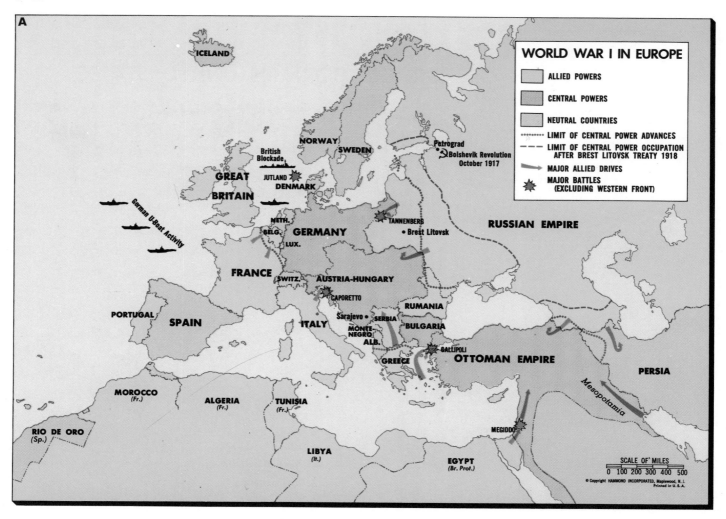

A

ICELAND

NORWAY
SWEDEN

British
Blockade
GREAT
BRITAIN
JUTLAND
DENMARK

German U-Boat Activity

Petrograd
Bolshevik Revolution
October 1917

RUSSIAN EMPIRE

NETH.
BELG.
GERMANY
LUX.

TANNENBERG
• Brest Litovsk

FRANCE

SWITZ.
AUSTRIA-HUNGARY

CAPORETTO

PORTUGAL
SPAIN
ITALY

Sarajevo •
MONTE-
NEGRO
ALB.
SERBIA
RUMANIA
BULGARIA

GALLIPOLI

GREECE
OTTOMAN EMPIRE

PERSIA

Mesopotamia

MOROCCO
ALGERIA
(Fr.)
TUNISIA
(Fr.)

RIO DE ORO
(Sp.)

LIBYA
(It.)
EGYPT
(Br. Prot.)

MEGIDDO

WORLD WAR I IN EUROPE

- ALLIED POWERS
- CENTRAL POWERS
- NEUTRAL COUNTRIES
- ········· LIMIT OF CENTRAL POWER ADVANCES
- ——— LIMIT OF CENTRAL POWER OCCUPATION AFTER BREST LITOVSK TREATY 1918
- ➤ MAJOR ALLIED DRIVES
- ✴ MAJOR BATTLES (EXCLUDING WESTERN FRONT)

SCALE OF MILES
0 100 200 300 400 500

© Copyright HAMMOND INCORPORATED, Maplewood, N.J.
Printed in U.S.A.

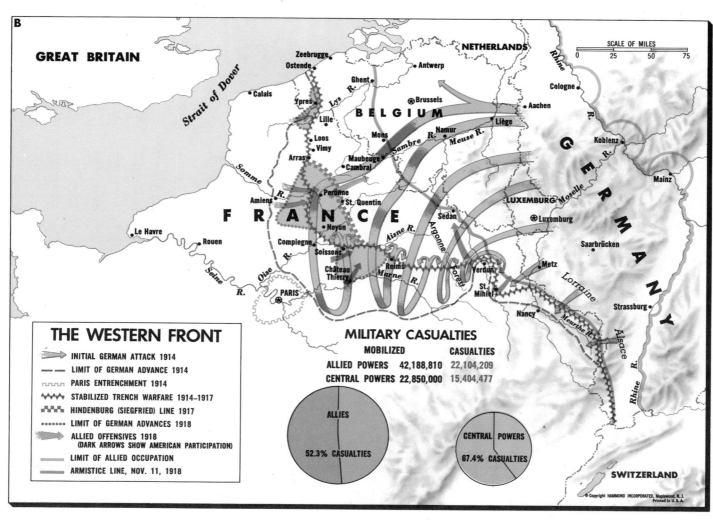

B

SCALE OF MILES
0   25   50   75

GREAT BRITAIN

NETHERLANDS

Rhine

Strait of Dover

Zeebrugge
Ostende
• Antwerp
Ghent •
• Calais
Ypres
Lys R.
• Brussels
BELGIUM
Cologne

Lille
Mons •
Namur
Liège
Aachen

Loos
Vimy
Maubeuge
• Cambrai
Sambre R.
Meuse R.

Koblenz

Arras

Somme R.
Amiens
Péronne
• St. Quentin
Sedan
LUXEMBURG
Moselle

GERMANY

Mainz

Le Havre
Rouen
Compiègne
Noyon
Aisne R.
Argonne Forest
⊕ Luxemburg

Soissons
Château
Thierry
Reims
Marne R.
Verdun
St. Mihiel
Metz
Saarbrücken

Seine R.
Oise R.
⊕ PARIS
FRANCE

Nancy
Lorraine
Meurthe R.
Strassburg

Rhine R.
Alsace

SWITZERLAND

THE WESTERN FRONT

- ➤ INITIAL GERMAN ATTACK 1914
- ——— LIMIT OF GERMAN ADVANCE 1914
- ⌇⌇⌇ PARIS ENTRENCHMENT 1914
- ◊◊◊ STABILIZED TRENCH WARFARE 1914–1917
- ▨▨▨ HINDENBURG (SIEGFRIED) LINE 1917
- ········· LIMIT OF GERMAN ADVANCES 1918
- ➤ ALLIED OFFENSIVES 1918 (DARK ARROWS SHOW AMERICAN PARTICIPATION)
- ——— LIMIT OF ALLIED OCCUPATION
- ——— ARMISTICE LINE, NOV. 11, 1918

MILITARY CASUALTIES

	MOBILIZED	CASUALTIES
ALLIED POWERS	42,188,810	22,104,209
CENTRAL POWERS	22,850,000	15,404,477

ALLIES
52.3% CASUALTIES

CENTRAL POWERS
67.4% CASUALTIES

© Copyright HAMMOND INCORPORATED, Maplewood, N.J.
Printed in U.S.A.

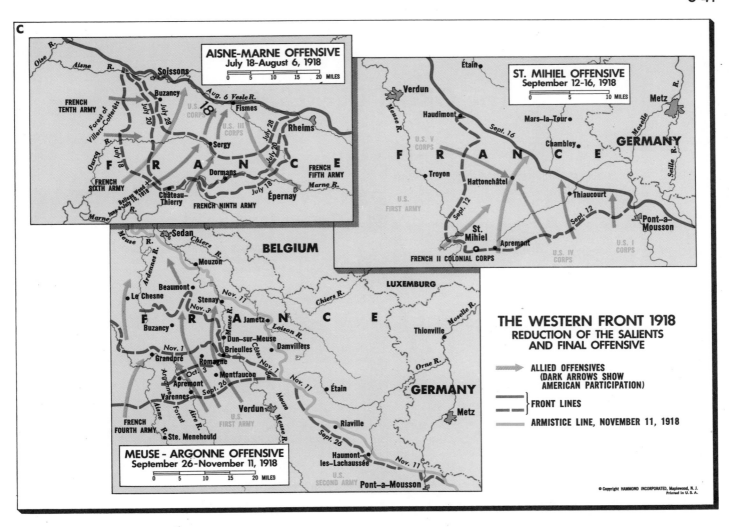

A

THE GREAT DEPRESSION

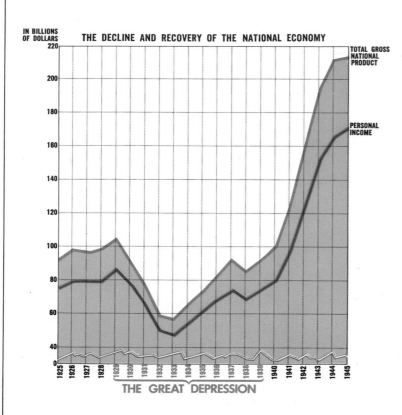

THE DECLINE AND RECOVERY OF THE NATIONAL ECONOMY

IN BILLIONS OF DOLLARS

TOTAL GROSS NATIONAL PRODUCT

PERSONAL INCOME

THE GREAT DEPRESSION

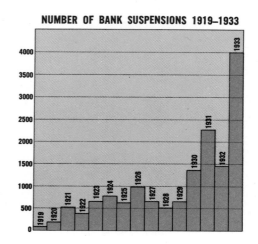

NUMBER OF BANK SUSPENSIONS 1919–1933

UNEMPLOYMENT

THE UNEMPLOYED AS A PERCENT OF THE CIVILIAN LABOR FORCE

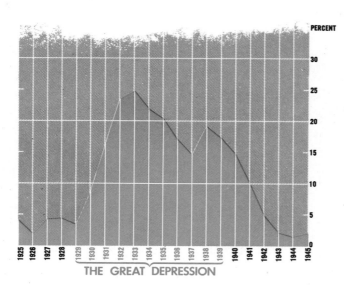

PERCENT

THE GREAT DEPRESSION

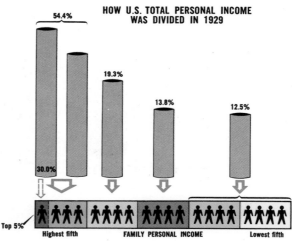

HOW U.S. TOTAL PERSONAL INCOME WAS DIVIDED IN 1929

54.4%

30.0%

19.3%

13.8%

12.5%

Top 5%

Highest fifth   FAMILY PERSONAL INCOME   Lowest fifth

HOURS WORKED IN MANUFACTURING (1925–1945)
(WEEKLY AVERAGE)

HOURS

Source: *Historical Statistics of the United States*

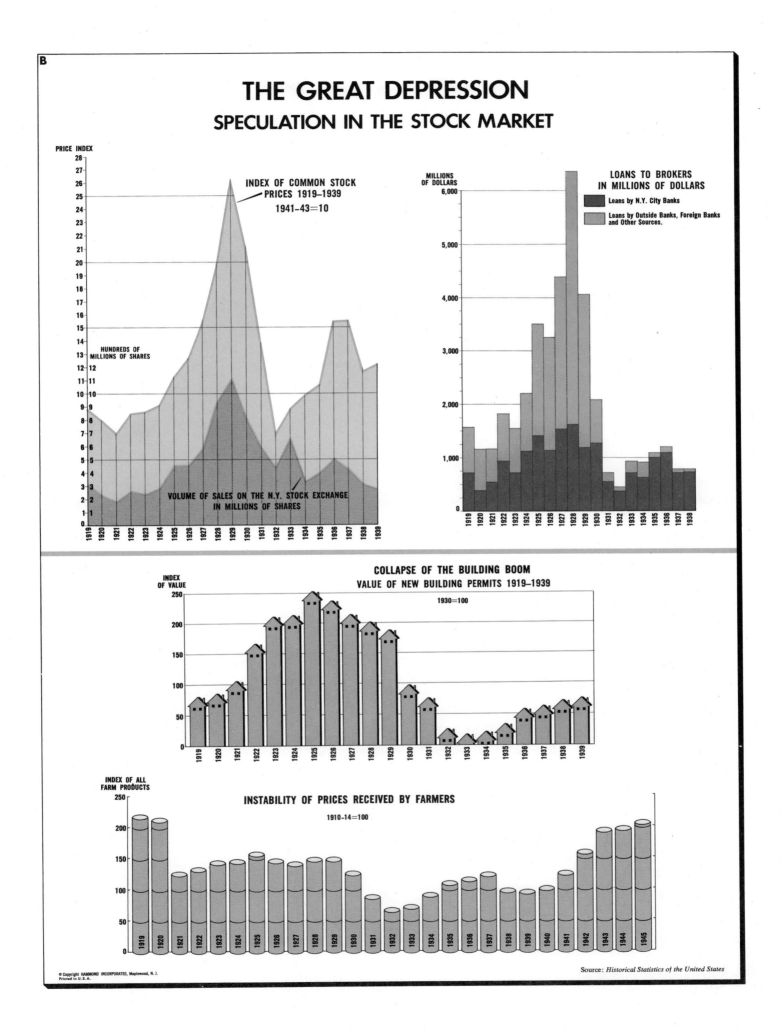

B

THE GREAT DEPRESSION
SPECULATION IN THE STOCK MARKET

PRICE INDEX

INDEX OF COMMON STOCK
PRICES 1919–1939
1941–43=10

HUNDREDS OF
MILLIONS OF SHARES

VOLUME OF SALES ON THE N.Y. STOCK EXCHANGE
IN MILLIONS OF SHARES

MILLIONS
OF DOLLARS

LOANS TO BROKERS
IN MILLIONS OF DOLLARS

Loans by N.Y. City Banks

Loans by Outside Banks, Foreign Banks
and Other Sources.

COLLAPSE OF THE BUILDING BOOM
VALUE OF NEW BUILDING PERMITS 1919–1939

INDEX
OF VALUE

1930=100

INDEX OF ALL
FARM PRODUCTS

INSTABILITY OF PRICES RECEIVED BY FARMERS

1910–14=100

© Copyright HAMMOND INCORPORATED, Maplewood, N.J.
Printed in U.S.A.

Source: *Historical Statistics of the United States*

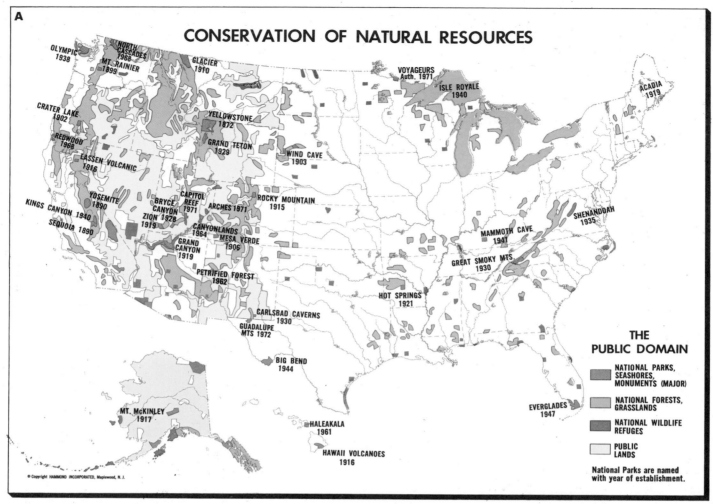

A

CONSERVATION OF NATURAL RESOURCES

THE PUBLIC DOMAIN

- NATIONAL PARKS, SEASHORES, MONUMENTS (MAJOR)
- NATIONAL FORESTS, GRASSLANDS
- NATIONAL WILDLIFE REFUGES
- PUBLIC LANDS

National Parks are named with year of establishment.

© Copyright HAMMOND INCORPORATED, Maplewood, N.J.

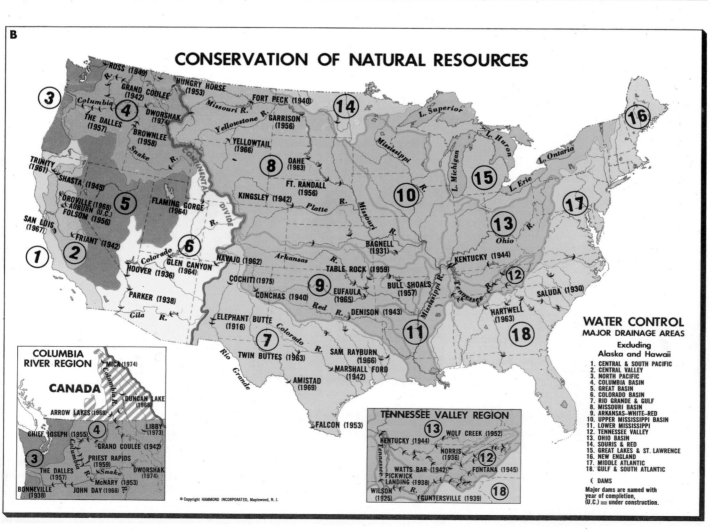

B

CONSERVATION OF NATURAL RESOURCES

WATER CONTROL
MAJOR DRAINAGE AREAS
Excluding Alaska and Hawaii

1. CENTRAL & SOUTH PACIFIC
2. CENTRAL VALLEY
3. NORTH PACIFIC
4. COLUMBIA BASIN
5. GREAT BASIN
6. COLORADO BASIN
7. RIO GRANDE & GULF
8. MISSOURI BASIN
9. ARKANSAS–WHITE–RED
10. UPPER MISSISSIPPI BASIN
11. LOWER MISSISSIPPI
12. TENNESSEE VALLEY
13. OHIO BASIN
14. SOURIS & RED
15. GREAT LAKES & ST. LAWRENCE
16. NEW ENGLAND
17. MIDDLE ATLANTIC
18. GULF & SOUTH ATLANTIC

⟨ DAMS

Major dams are named with year of completion.
(U.C.) = under construction.

COLUMBIA RIVER REGION

CANADA

TENNESSEE VALLEY REGION

© Copyright HAMMOND INCORPORATED, Maplewood, N.J.

C

CONSERVATION OF NATURAL RESOURCES

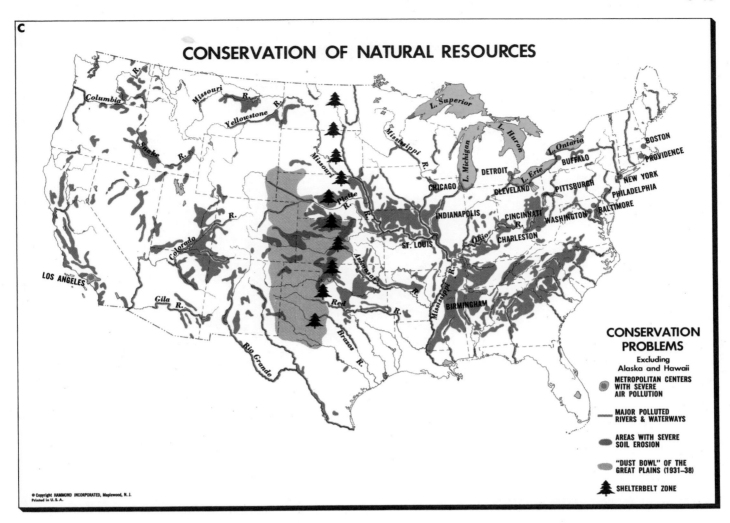

CONSERVATION PROBLEMS

Excluding Alaska and Hawaii

METROPOLITAN CENTERS WITH SEVERE AIR POLLUTION

MAJOR POLLUTED RIVERS & WATERWAYS

AREAS WITH SEVERE SOIL EROSION

"DUST BOWL" OF THE GREAT PLAINS (1931–38)

SHELTERBELT ZONE

D

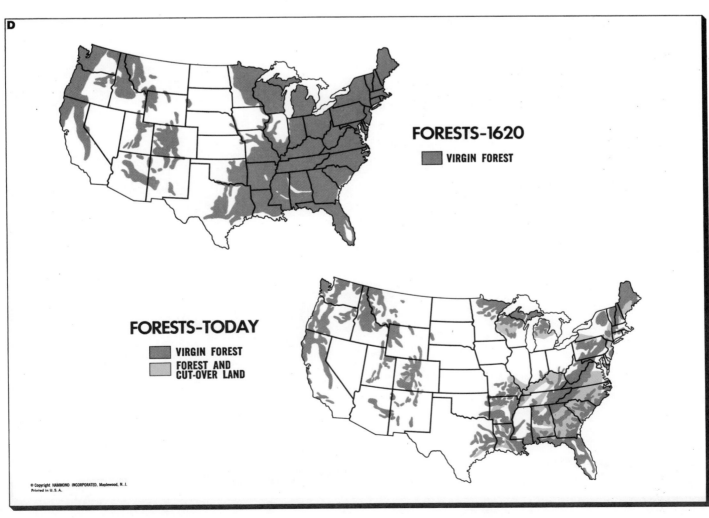

FORESTS-1620

VIRGIN FOREST

FORESTS-TODAY

VIRGIN FOREST

FOREST AND CUT-OVER LAND

A

GERMAN EXPANSION 1935-1939*

SCALE OF MILES

0   100   200   300   400

- Germany 1933
- Area gained by Plebiscite 1935
- Areas annexed 1938
- Area annexed 1939
- German Protectorates

*To Invasion of Poland Sept. 1, 1939

© Copyright HAMMOND INCORPORATED. Maplewood, N.J.
Printed in U.S.A.

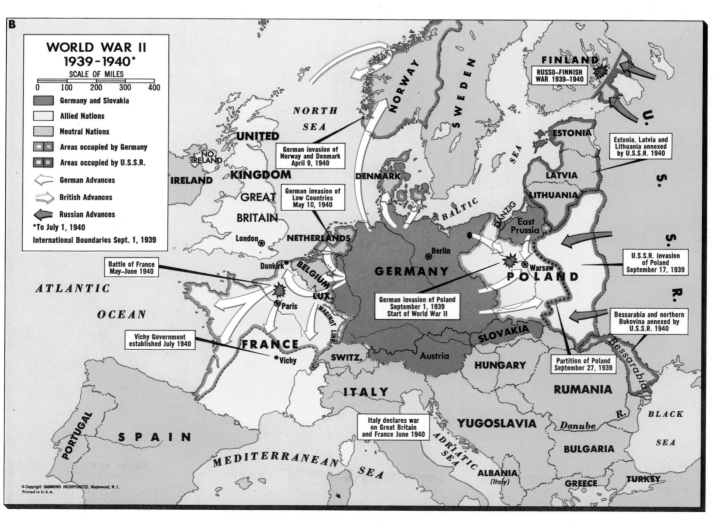

B

WORLD WAR II 1939-1940*

SCALE OF MILES

0   100   200   300   400

- Germany and Slovakia
- Allied Nations
- Neutral Nations
- Areas occupied by Germany
- Areas occupied by U.S.S.R.
- German Advances
- British Advances
- Russian Advances

*To July 1, 1940

International Boundaries Sept. 1, 1939

© Copyright HAMMOND INCORPORATED. Maplewood, N.J.
Printed in U.S.A.

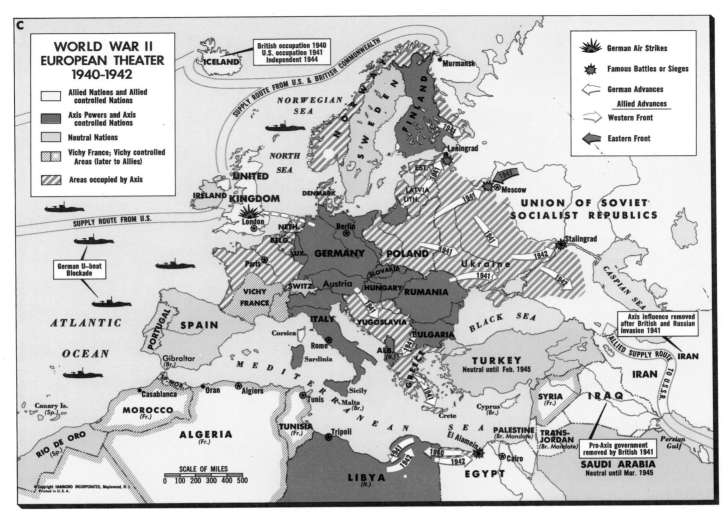

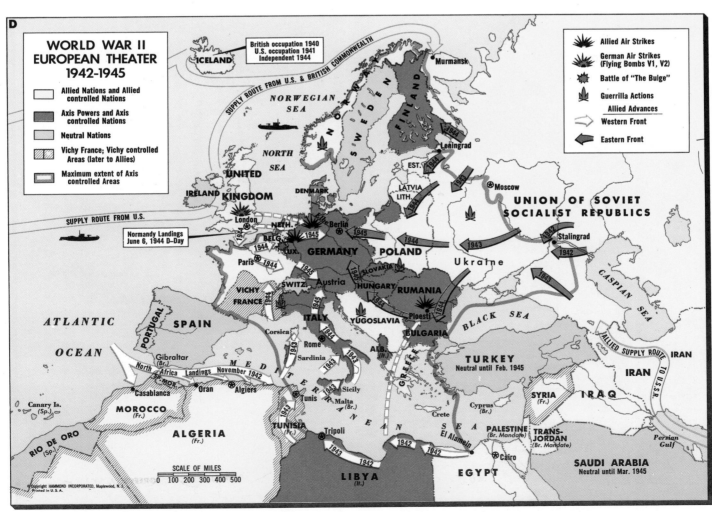

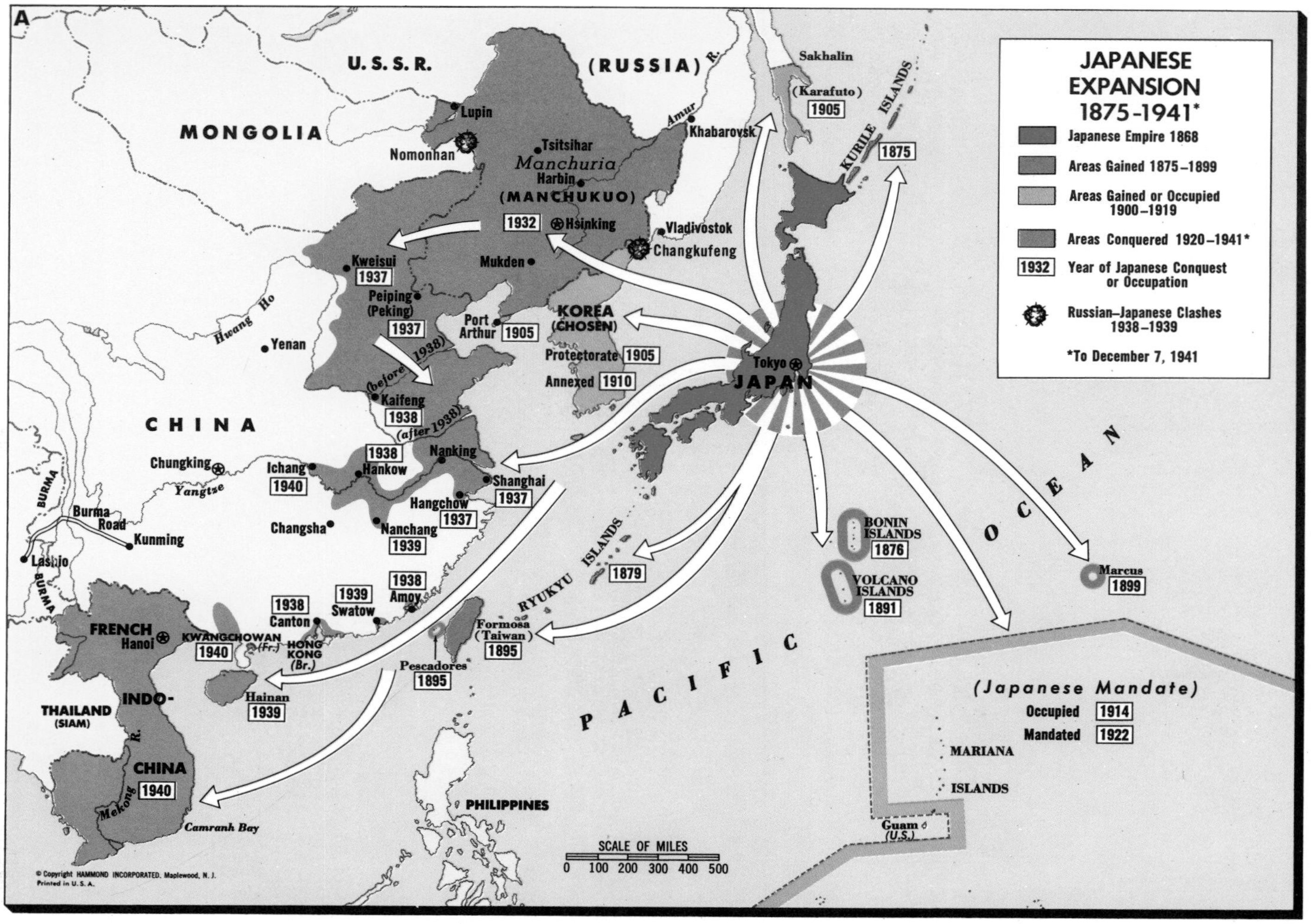
A
JAPANESE EXPANSION 1875-1941*
Japanese Empire 1868
Areas Gained 1875–1899
Areas Gained or Occupied 1900–1919
Areas Conquered 1920–1941*
1932 Year of Japanese Conquest or Occupation
Russian–Japanese Clashes 1938–1939
*To December 7, 1941
U. S. S. R.
(RUSSIA)
MONGOLIA
Lupin
Nomonhan
Tsitsihar
Manchuria
Harbin
(MANCHUKUO)
1932
Hsinking
Mukden
Amur R.
Khabarovsk
Vladivostok
Changkufeng
Sakhalin
(Karafuto)
1905
KURILE ISLANDS
1875
Kweisui
1937
Peiping (Peking)
1937
Hwang Ho
Yenan
Port Arthur
1905
KOREA (CHOSEN)
Protectorate 1905
Annexed 1910
(before 1938)
Kaifeng
1938
(after 1938)
Tokyo
JAPAN
CHINA
Chungking
Yangtze
Ichang
1940
1938
Hankow
Nanking
Shanghai
1937
Hangchow
1937
Changsha
Nanchang
1939
BURMA
Burma Road
Kunming
Lashio
BURMA
1938
Amoy
1939
Swatow
1938
Canton
RYUKYU ISLANDS
1879
Formosa (Taiwan)
1895
Pescadores
1895
BONIN ISLANDS
1876
VOLCANO ISLANDS
1891
Marcus
1899
OCEAN
PACIFIC
FRENCH
Hanoi
KWANGCHOWAN (Fr.)
1940
HONG KONG (Br.)
Hainan
1939
THAILAND (SIAM)
INDO-
CHINA
1940
Mekong R.
Camranh Bay
PHILIPPINES
(Japanese Mandate)
Occupied 1914
Mandated 1922
MARIANA
ISLANDS
Guam (U.S.)
SCALE OF MILES
0 100 200 300 400 500
© Copyright HAMMOND INCORPORATED, Maplewood, N. J.
Printed in U. S. A.

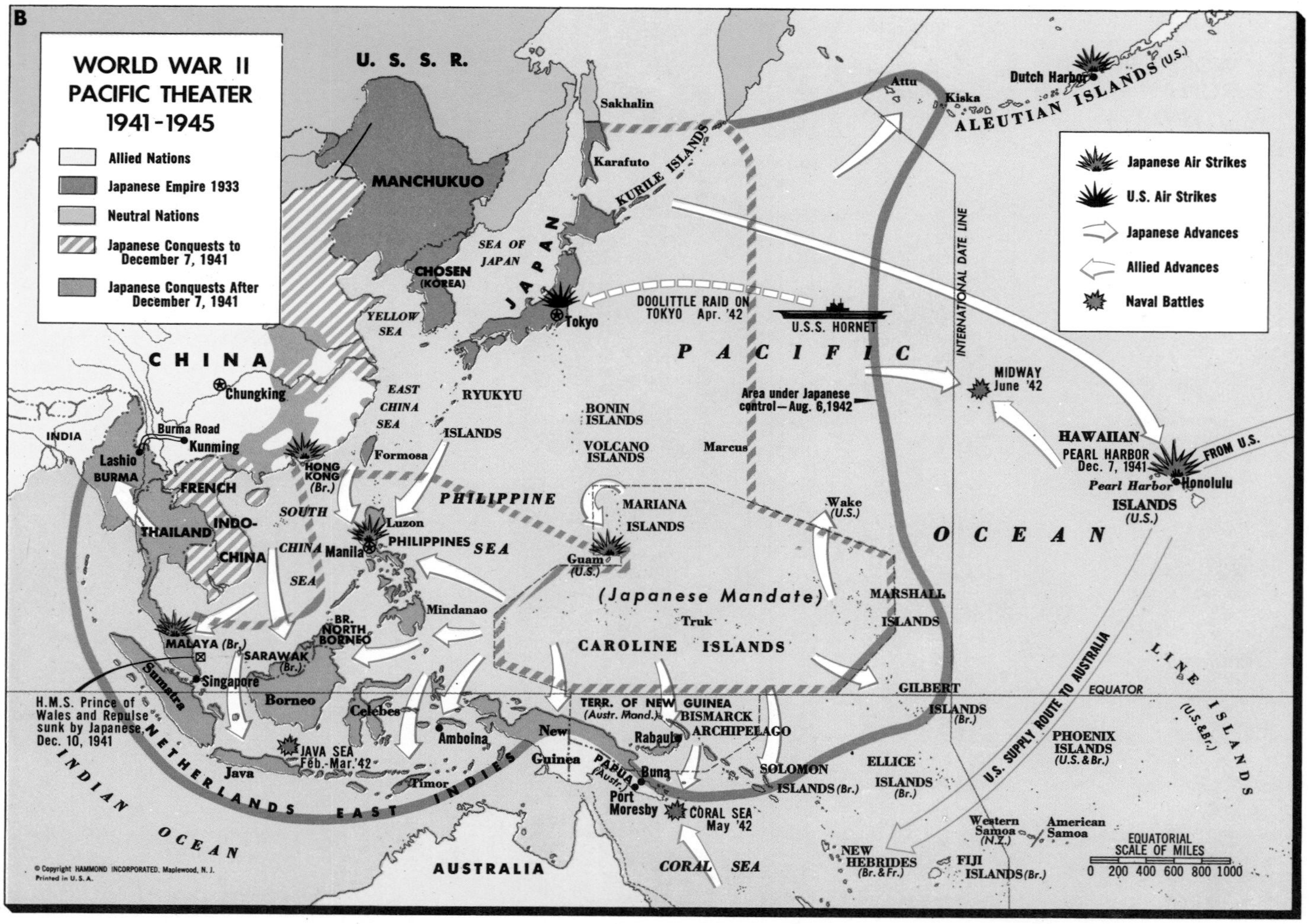
B
WORLD WAR II PACIFIC THEATER 1941-1945
Allied Nations
Japanese Empire 1933
Neutral Nations
Japanese Conquests to December 7, 1941
Japanese Conquests After December 7, 1941
Japanese Air Strikes
U.S. Air Strikes
Japanese Advances
Allied Advances
Naval Battles
U. S. S. R.
Sakhalin
Karafuto
KURILE ISLANDS
MANCHUKUO
CHOSEN (KOREA)
SEA OF JAPAN
JAPAN
Tokyo
YELLOW SEA
DOOLITTLE RAID ON TOKYO Apr. '42
U.S.S. HORNET
Attu
Kiska
Dutch Harbor
ALEUTIAN ISLANDS (U.S.)
INTERNATIONAL DATE LINE
PACIFIC
OCEAN
MIDWAY June '42
Area under Japanese control—Aug. 6,1942
CHINA
Chungking
INDIA
Burma Road
Kunming
Lashio
BURMA
FRENCH
INDO-
CHINA
THAILAND
EAST CHINA SEA
RYUKYU ISLANDS
Formosa
HONG KONG (Br.)
BONIN ISLANDS
VOLCANO ISLANDS
Marcus
HAWAIIAN
PEARL HARBOR Dec. 7, 1941
Pearl Harbor
Honolulu
ISLANDS (U.S.)
FROM U.S.
PHILIPPINE SEA
SOUTH CHINA SEA
Luzon
PHILIPPINES
Manila
MARIANA ISLANDS
Guam (U.S.)
Wake (U.S.)
(Japanese Mandate)
Truk
CAROLINE ISLANDS
MARSHALL ISLANDS
Mindanao
BR. NORTH BORNEO
SARAWAK (Br.)
MALAYA (Br.)
Singapore
Sumatra
Borneo
Celebes
Amboina
H.M.S. Prince of Wales and Repulse sunk by Japanese Dec. 10, 1941
JAVA SEA Feb.-Mar. '42
Java
Timor
NETHERLANDS EAST INDIES
TERR. OF NEW GUINEA (Austr. Mand.)
BISMARCK ARCHIPELAGO
Rabaul
New Guinea
PAPUA (Austr.)
Buna
Port Moresby
CORAL SEA May '42
SOLOMON ISLANDS (Br.)
ELLICE ISLANDS (Br.)
GILBERT ISLANDS (Br.)
EQUATOR
PHOENIX ISLANDS (U.S. & Br.)
LINE ISLANDS (U.S.&Br.)
U.S. SUPPLY ROUTE TO AUSTRALIA
Western Samoa (N.Z.)
American Samoa
NEW HEBRIDES (Br. & Fr.)
FIJI ISLANDS (Br.)
INDIAN OCEAN
AUSTRALIA
CORAL SEA
EQUATORIAL SCALE OF MILES
0 200 400 600 800 1000
© Copyright HAMMOND INCORPORATED, Maplewood, N. J.
Printed in U. S. A.

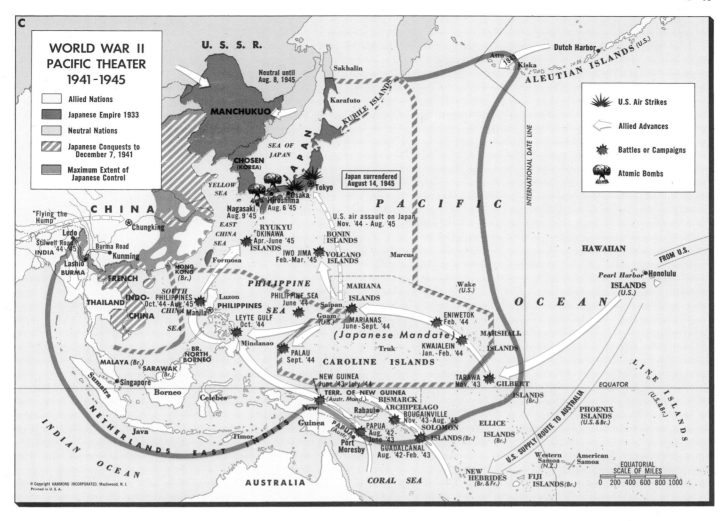

C

WORLD WAR II PACIFIC THEATER 1941-1945

- Allied Nations
- Japanese Empire 1933
- Neutral Nations
- Japanese Conquests to December 7, 1941
- Maximum Extent of Japanese Control

- ☀ U.S. Air Strikes
- ⇦ Allied Advances
- ✹ Battles or Campaigns
- ☢ Atomic Bombs

U. S. S. R.

Neutral until Aug. 8, 1945

Dutch Harbor

Attu 1942

Kiska

ALEUTIAN ISLANDS (U.S.)

Sakhalin

Karafuto

MANCHUKUO

KURILE ISLANDS

SEA OF JAPAN

CHOSEN (KOREA)

Japan surrendered August 14, 1945

INTERNATIONAL DATE LINE

P A C I F I C

CHINA

YELLOW SEA

Osaka

Tokyo

Hiroshima Aug. 6 '45

Nagasaki Aug. 9 '45

EAST CHINA SEA

OKINAWA Apr.-June '45

RYUKYU ISLANDS

BONIN ISLANDS

U.S. air assault on Japan Nov. '44 - Aug. '45

HAWAIIAN

"Flying the Hump"

Chungking

Ledo

Stilwell Road '44-'45

INDIA

Burma Road

Kunming

Lashio

BURMA

FRENCH

THAILAND

INDO-CHINA

HONG KONG (Br.)

Formosa

IWO JIMA Feb.-Mar. '45

VOLCANO ISLANDS

Marcus

Wake (U.S.)

Pearl Harbor

Honolulu

FROM U.S.

ISLANDS (U.S.)

SOUTH PHILIPPINES Oct.'44-Aug.'45

Luzon

Manila

PHILIPPINES

LEYTE GULF Oct. '44

PHILIPPINE SEA June '44

MARIANA ISLANDS

Saipan

Guam (U.S.)

PHILIPPINE SEA

MARIANAS June-Sept. '44

ENIWETOK Feb. '44

MARSHALL

Mindanao

PALAU Sept. '44

Truk

KWAJALEIN Jan.-Feb. '44

ISLANDS

(Japanese Mandate)

CAROLINE ISLANDS

EQUATOR

LINE

MALAYA (Br.)

SARAWAK (Br.)

BR. NORTH BORNEO

Singapore

Borneo

Celebes

NETHERLANDS EAST INDIES

NEW GUINEA June '43-July '44

TERR. OF NEW GUINEA (Austr. Mand.)

BISMARCK ARCHIPELAGO

New Guinea

Rabaul

BOUGAINVILLE Nov. '43-Aug. '45

TARAWA Nov. '43

GILBERT ISLANDS (Br.)

PHOENIX ISLANDS (U.S.&Br.)

ISLANDS (U.S.&Br.)

INDIAN OCEAN

Sumatra

Java

Timor

PAPUA (Austr.)

Port Moresby

PAPUA Aug. '42-June '43

SOLOMON ISLANDS (Br.)

GUADALCANAL Aug. '42-Feb. '43

ELLICE ISLANDS (Br.)

U.S. SUPPLY ROUTE TO AUSTRALIA

Western Samoa (N.Z.)

American Samoa

EQUATORIAL SCALE OF MILES

0 200 400 600 800 1000

AUSTRALIA

CORAL SEA

NEW HEBRIDES (Br. & Fr.)

FIJI ISLANDS (Br.)

© Copyright HAMMOND INCORPORATED, Maplewood, N.J.
Printed in U.S.A.

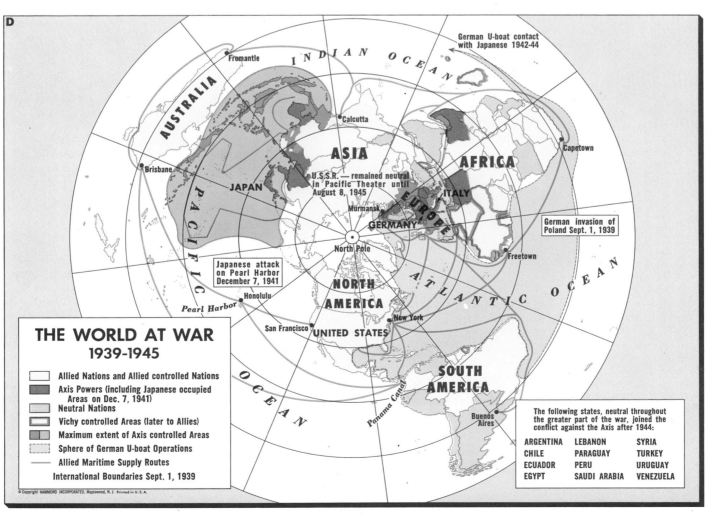

D

German U-boat contact with Japanese 1942-44

INDIAN OCEAN

Fremantle

Calcutta

Capetown

AUSTRALIA

Brisbane

PACIFIC

ASIA

JAPAN

U.S.S.R. — remained neutral in Pacific Theater until August 8, 1945

AFRICA

EUROPE

ITALY

German invasion of Poland Sept. 1, 1939

Murmansk

GERMANY

Freetown

Japanese attack on Pearl Harbor December 7, 1941

North Pole

NORTH AMERICA

ATLANTIC OCEAN

Pearl Harbor

Honolulu

San Francisco

UNITED STATES

New York

THE WORLD AT WAR
1939-1945

- Allied Nations and Allied controlled Nations
- Axis Powers (including Japanese occupied Areas on Dec. 7, 1941)
- Neutral Nations
- Vichy controlled Areas (later to Allies)
- Maximum extent of Axis controlled Areas
- Sphere of German U-boat Operations
- — Allied Maritime Supply Routes
- International Boundaries Sept. 1, 1939

OCEAN

Panama Canal

SOUTH AMERICA

Buenos Aires

The following states, neutral throughout the greater part of the war, joined the conflict against the Axis after 1944:

ARGENTINA	LEBANON	SYRIA
CHILE	PARAGUAY	TURKEY
ECUADOR	PERU	URUGUAY
EGYPT	SAUDI ARABIA	VENEZUELA

© Copyright HAMMOND INCORPORATED, Maplewood, N.J. Printed in U.S.A.

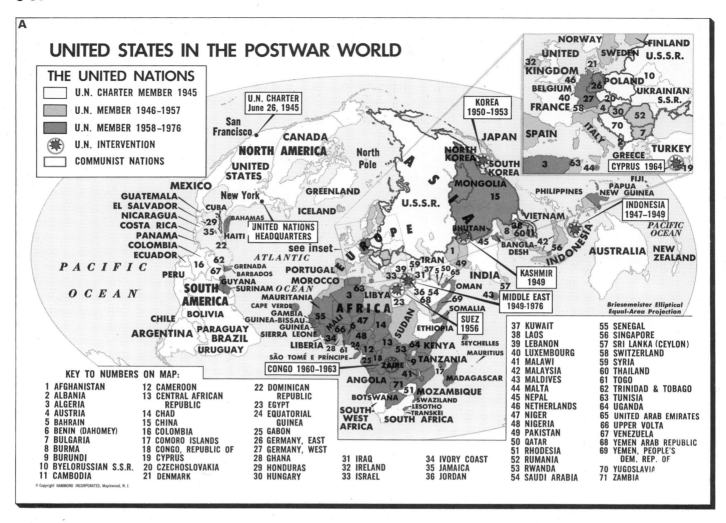

A. UNITED STATES IN THE POSTWAR WORLD

THE UNITED NATIONS

- U.N. CHARTER MEMBER 1945
- U.N. MEMBER 1946–1957
- U.N. MEMBER 1958–1976
- U.N. INTERVENTION
- COMMUNIST NATIONS

KEY TO NUMBERS ON MAP:

1 AFGHANISTAN	12 CAMEROON	22 DOMINICAN REPUBLIC
2 ALBANIA	13 CENTRAL AFRICAN REPUBLIC	23 EGYPT
3 ALGERIA	14 CHAD	24 EQUATORIAL GUINEA
4 AUSTRIA	15 CHINA	25 GABON
5 BAHRAIN	16 COLOMBIA	26 GERMANY, EAST
6 BENIN (DAHOMEY)	17 COMORO ISLANDS	27 GERMANY, WEST
7 BULGARIA	18 CONGO, REPUBLIC OF	28 GHANA
8 BURMA	19 CYPRUS	29 HONDURAS
9 BURUNDI	20 CZECHOSLOVAKIA	30 HUNGARY
10 BYELORUSSIAN S.S.R.	21 DENMARK	
11 CAMBODIA		

31 IRAQ	34 IVORY COAST	37 KUWAIT	55 SENEGAL
32 IRELAND	35 JAMAICA	38 LAOS	56 SINGAPORE
33 ISRAEL	36 JORDAN	39 LEBANON	57 SRI LANKA (CEYLON)
		40 LUXEMBOURG	58 SWITZERLAND
		41 MALAWI	59 SYRIA
		42 MALAYSIA	60 THAILAND
		43 MALDIVES	61 TOGO
		44 MALTA	62 TRINIDAD & TOBAGO
		45 NEPAL	63 TUNISIA
		46 NETHERLANDS	64 UGANDA
		47 NIGER	65 UNITED ARAB EMIRATES
		48 NIGERIA	66 UPPER VOLTA
		49 PAKISTAN	67 VENEZUELA
		50 QATAR	68 YEMEN ARAB REPUBLIC
		51 RHODESIA	69 YEMEN, PEOPLE'S DEM. REP. OF
		52 RUMANIA	70 YUGOSLAVIA
		53 RWANDA	71 ZAMBIA
		54 SAUDI ARABIA	

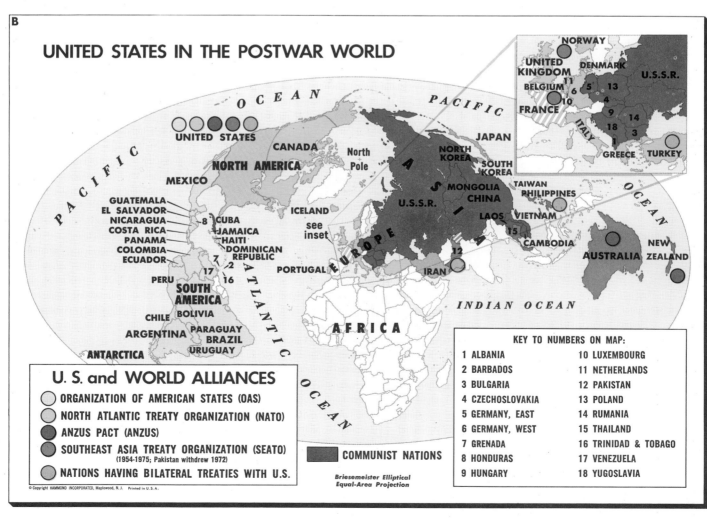

B. UNITED STATES IN THE POSTWAR WORLD

U.S. and WORLD ALLIANCES

- ORGANIZATION OF AMERICAN STATES (OAS)
- NORTH ATLANTIC TREATY ORGANIZATION (NATO)
- ANZUS PACT (ANZUS)
- SOUTHEAST ASIA TREATY ORGANIZATION (SEATO) (1954–1975; Pakistan withdrew 1972)
- NATIONS HAVING BILATERAL TREATIES WITH U.S.
- COMMUNIST NATIONS

KEY TO NUMBERS ON MAP:

1 ALBANIA	10 LUXEMBOURG
2 BARBADOS	11 NETHERLANDS
3 BULGARIA	12 PAKISTAN
4 CZECHOSLOVAKIA	13 POLAND
5 GERMANY, EAST	14 RUMANIA
6 GERMANY, WEST	15 THAILAND
7 GRENADA	16 TRINIDAD & TOBAGO
8 HONDURAS	17 VENEZUELA
9 HUNGARY	18 YUGOSLAVIA

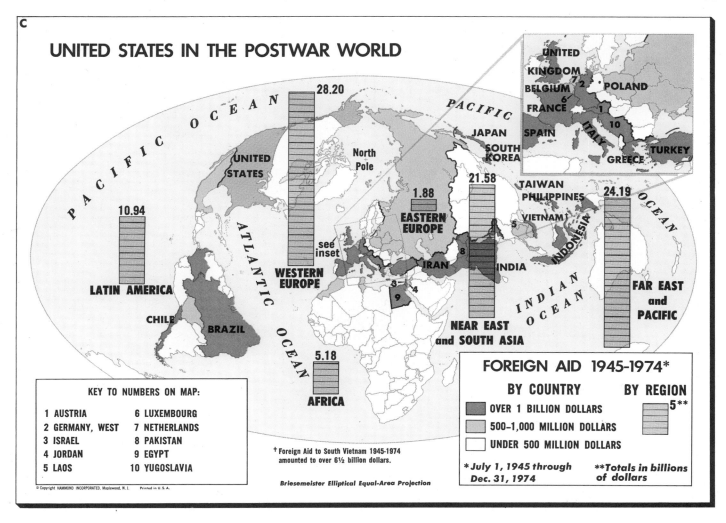

C

UNITED STATES IN THE POSTWAR WORLD

KEY TO NUMBERS ON MAP:

1 AUSTRIA	6 LUXEMBOURG
2 GERMANY, WEST	7 NETHERLANDS
3 ISRAEL	8 PAKISTAN
4 JORDAN	9 EGYPT
5 LAOS	10 YUGOSLAVIA

© Copyright HAMMOND INCORPORATED, Maplewood, N. J.   Printed in U.S.A.

† Foreign Aid to South Vietnam 1945-1974
amounted to over 6½ billion dollars.

Briesemeister Elliptical Equal-Area Projection

FOREIGN AID 1945-1974*

BY COUNTRY

- ▨ OVER 1 BILLION DOLLARS
- ▨ 500–1,000 MILLION DOLLARS
- ☐ UNDER 500 MILLION DOLLARS

BY REGION

▨ 5**

*July 1, 1945 through Dec. 31, 1974

**Totals in billions of dollars

Map labels: UNITED STATES, EASTERN EUROPE 1.88, WESTERN EUROPE 28.20, LATIN AMERICA 10.94, CHILE, BRAZIL, AFRICA 5.18, NEAR EAST and SOUTH ASIA 21.58, IRAN, INDIA, FAR EAST and PACIFIC 24.19, JAPAN, SOUTH KOREA, TAIWAN, PHILIPPINES, VIETNAM, INDONESIA, North Pole, see inset

Inset labels: UNITED KINGDOM, BELGIUM, FRANCE, SPAIN, POLAND, ITALY, GREECE, TURKEY

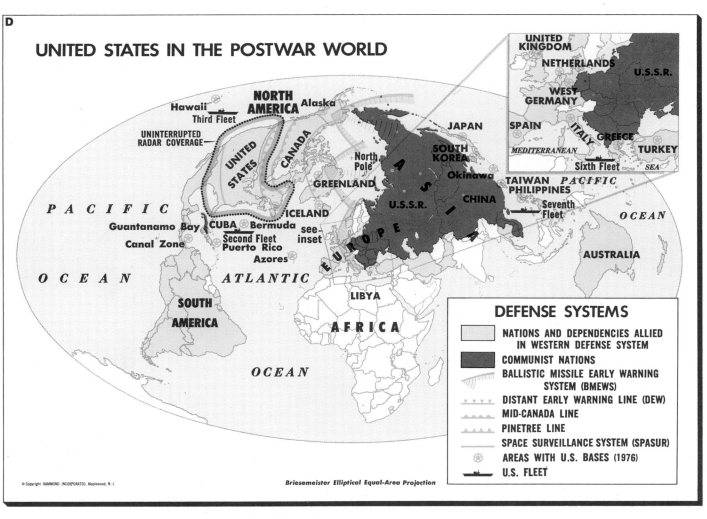

D

UNITED STATES IN THE POSTWAR WORLD

© Copyright HAMMOND INCORPORATED, Maplewood, N. J.

Briesemeister Elliptical Equal-Area Projection

DEFENSE SYSTEMS

- ☐ NATIONS AND DEPENDENCIES ALLIED IN WESTERN DEFENSE SYSTEM
- ■ COMMUNIST NATIONS
- ⋰⋰ BALLISTIC MISSILE EARLY WARNING SYSTEM (BMEWS)
- ▽▽▽▽ DISTANT EARLY WARNING LINE (DEW)
- ≈≈≈ MID-CANADA LINE
- ▲▲▲ PINETREE LINE
- ── SPACE SURVEILLANCE SYSTEM (SPASUR)
- ✷ AREAS WITH U.S. BASES (1976)
- ▬ U.S. FLEET

Map labels: NORTH AMERICA, Hawaii, Third Fleet, UNINTERRUPTED RADAR COVERAGE, UNITED STATES, CANADA, Alaska, Guantanamo Bay, Canal Zone, CUBA, Bermuda, Second Fleet, Puerto Rico, Azores, ICELAND, GREENLAND, North Pole, U.S.S.R., ASIA, EUROPE, JAPAN, SOUTH KOREA, Okinawa, CHINA, Seventh Fleet, TAIWAN, PHILIPPINES, SOUTH AMERICA, AFRICA, LIBYA, AUSTRALIA, see inset, PACIFIC OCEAN, ATLANTIC OCEAN

Inset labels: UNITED KINGDOM, NETHERLANDS, WEST GERMANY, SPAIN, U.S.S.R., ITALY, GREECE, TURKEY, MEDITERRANEAN SEA, Sixth Fleet

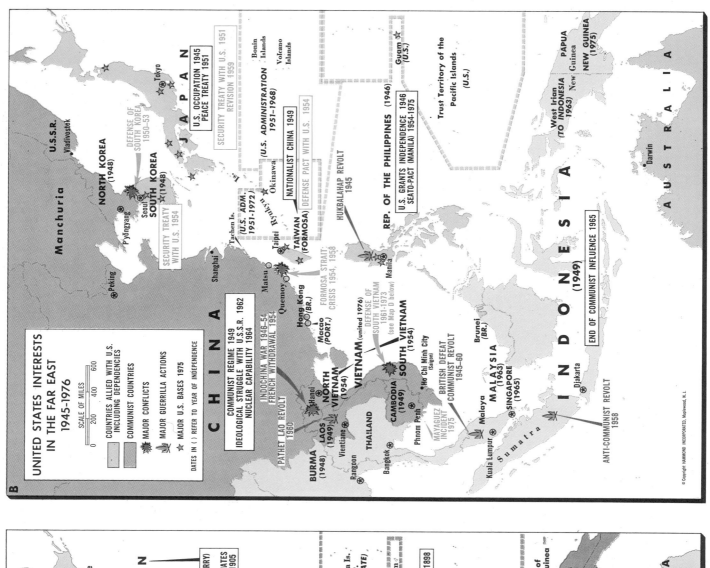

A

UNITED STATES INTERESTS IN THE FAR EAST 1854-1937

SCALE OF MILES
0 200 400 600

- U.S. DEPENDENCIES
- OTHER DEPENDENCIES
- MAJOR TREATY PORTS
- ✦ CONFLICTS INVOLVING U.S. FORCES

© Copyright HAMMOND INCORPORATED, Maplewood, N.J.
Printed in U.S.A.

RUSSIA (U.S.S.R.)

Vladivostok

INTERVENTION IN RUSSIAN CIVIL WAR 1918-20

Hakodate

J A P A N

Tokyo

Shimoda
Osaka

TREATY PORT AGREEMENT (PERRY) 1854-99
PRESIDENT T. ROOSEVELT MEDIATES IN RUSSIAN-JAPANESE WAR 1905

Manchuria (Manchukuo) (JAP.)

Mukden

Korea (Chosen) (JAP.)

Dairen (JAP.)
Weihwei (BR. UNTIL 1930)
Kiaochow (GER. UNTIL 1914)

Peking
Tientsin
BOXER REBELLION 1900

Nagasaki
PANAY INCIDENT 1937
Kyushu Islands (JAP.)

P A C I F I C

O C E A N

C H I N A

Chungking

Nanking
Hankow
Shanghai
Ningpo
Foochow
Amoy

JAPAN EXTENDS OCCUPATION OF CHINA 1937
OPEN DOOR POLICY 1899
STIMSON DOCTRINE 1932

Formosa (JAP.)

Nanning
Canton
Hong Kong (BR.)
Macao (PORT.)
Kwangchowan (FR.)

Mariana Is. (JAP. MANDATE)

Guam

CEDED BY SPAIN 1898

Caroline Islands (JAP. MANDATE)

Luzon

Manila

CEDED BY SPAIN 1898
MILITARY GOVERNMENT 1898-1901
JONES ACT 1916
COMMONWEALTH STATUS 1935

Philippine Islands

Mindanao

SPANISH-AMERICAN WAR, PHILIPPINES CAMPAIGN 1898

PHILIPPINE INSURRECTION 1899-1902

Terr. of New Guinea

New Guinea
Papua

S I A M
Bangkok
Burma (BR.)
Rangoon

French Indochina
Hanoi
Saigon

Malay States (BR.)
Singapore (BR.)

Br. North Borneo (BR.)
Brunei (BR.)
Sarawak (BR.)

Netherlands East Indies

Batavia
Surabaya

Timor (PORT.)

A U S T R A L I A

COMMONWEALTH STATUS 1901

I N D I A N

O C E A N

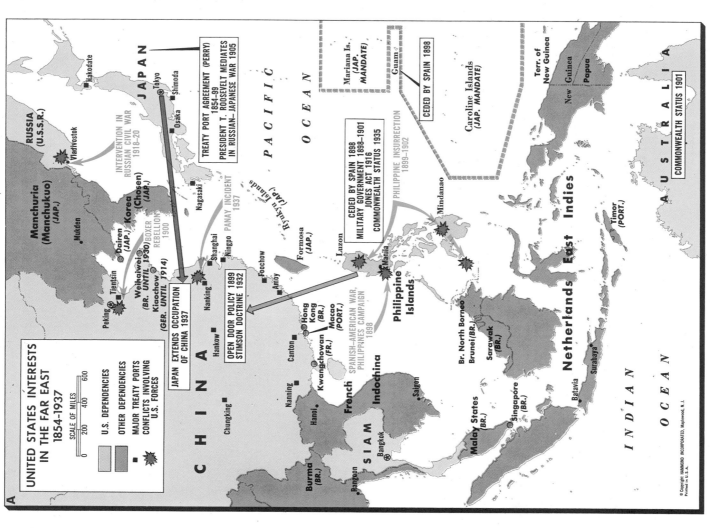

B

UNITED STATES INTERESTS IN THE FAR EAST 1945-1976

SCALE OF MILES
0 200 400 600

- COUNTRIES ALLIED WITH U.S. INCLUDING DEPENDENCIES
- COMMUNIST COUNTRIES
- ✦ MAJOR CONFLICTS
- MAJOR GUERRILLA ACTIONS
- ★ MAJOR U.S. BASES 1975

DATES IN ( ) REFER TO YEAR OF INDEPENDENCE

© Copyright HAMMOND INCORPORATED, Maplewood, N.J.

U.S.S.R.
Vladivostok

Manchuria

Peking

NORTH KOREA (1948)
P'yŏngyang

DEFENSE OF SOUTH KOREA 1950-53

SOUTH KOREA (1948)
Seoul

SECURITY TREATY WITH U.S. 1954

J A P A N
Tokyo

U.S. OCCUPATION 1945 PEACE TREATY 1951
SECURITY TREATY WITH U.S. 1951 REVISION 1959

Bonin Islands

Volcano Islands

(U.S. ADMINISTRATION 1951-1968)

Okinawa
(U.S. ADM. 1951-1972)
Ryukyu Is.

NATIONALIST CHINA 1949
DEFENSE PACT WITH U.S. 1954

Guam (U.S.) ★

Trust Territory of the Pacific Islands (U.S.)

PAPUA

NEW GUINEA New Guinea

NEW GUINEA (1975)

Darwin

C H I N A

Shanghai

COMMUNIST REGIME 1949
IDEOLOGICAL STRUGGLE WITH U.S.S.R. 1962
NUCLEAR CAPABILITY 1964

INDOCHINA WAR 1946-54 FRENCH WITHDRAWAL 1954

Tachen Is.
Matsu
Quemoy
Taipei
TAIWAN (FORMOSA)

FORMOSA STRAIT CRISIS 1954, 1958

Hong Kong (BR.)
Macao (PORT.)

HUKBALAHAP REVOLT 1945

REP. OF THE PHILIPPINES (1946)

Manila

U.S. GRANTS INDEPENDENCE 1946 SEATO-PACT (MANILA) 1954-1975

Hanoi
NORTH VIETNAM (1954)

PATHET LAO REVOLT 1960

BURMA (1948)
LAOS (1949)
Vientiane

THAILAND
Rangoon
Bangkok

CAMBODIA (1949)
Phnom Penh

VIETNAM (united 1976)

DEFENSE OF SOUTH VIETNAM 1961-1973 (see Map D below)

SOUTH VIETNAM (1954)
Ho Chi Minh City (Saigon)

MATAGUEZ INCIDENT 1975

BRITISH DEFEAT COMMUNIST REVOLT 1945-60

Malaya
MALAYSIA (1963)
Brunei (BR.)

Kuala Lumpur
SINGAPORE (1965)

Sumatra

I N D O N E S I A (1949)

Djakarta

ANTI-COMMUNIST REVOLT 1958

END OF COMMUNIST INFLUENCE 1965

West Irian 1963 (TO INDONESIA)

A U S T R A L I A

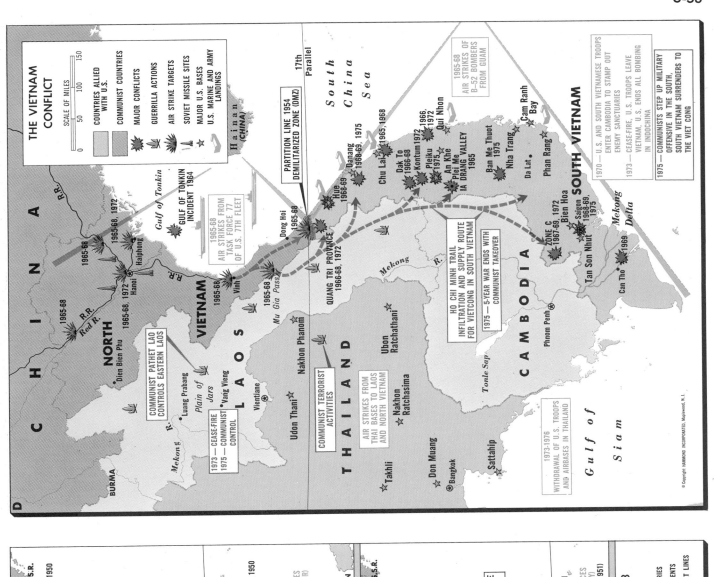

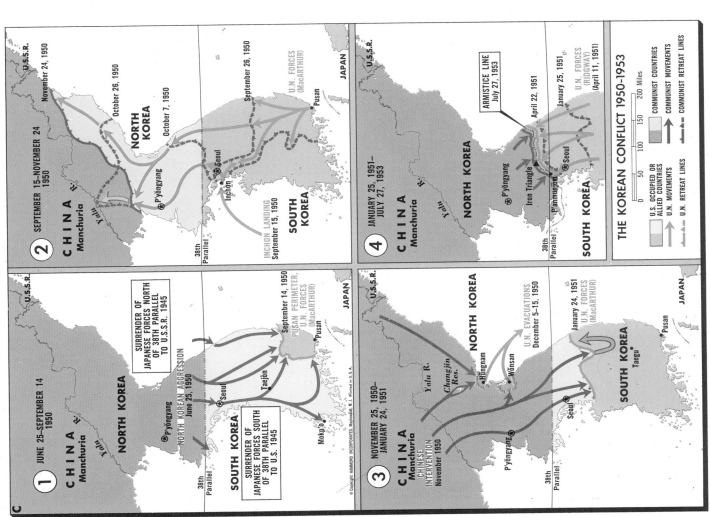

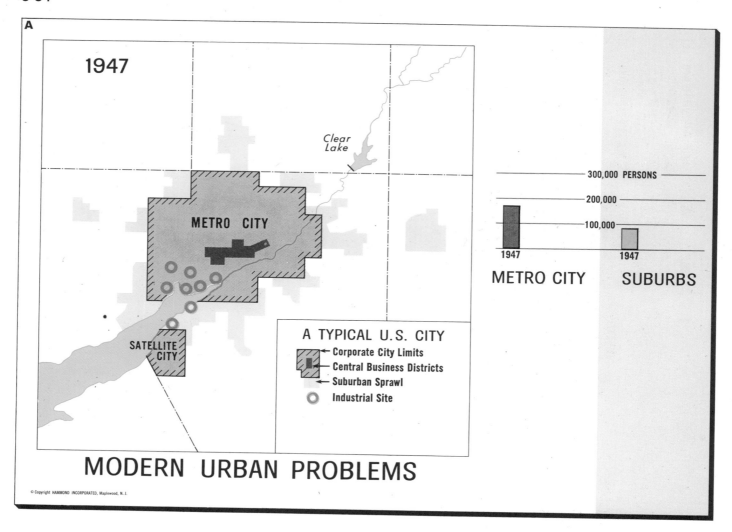

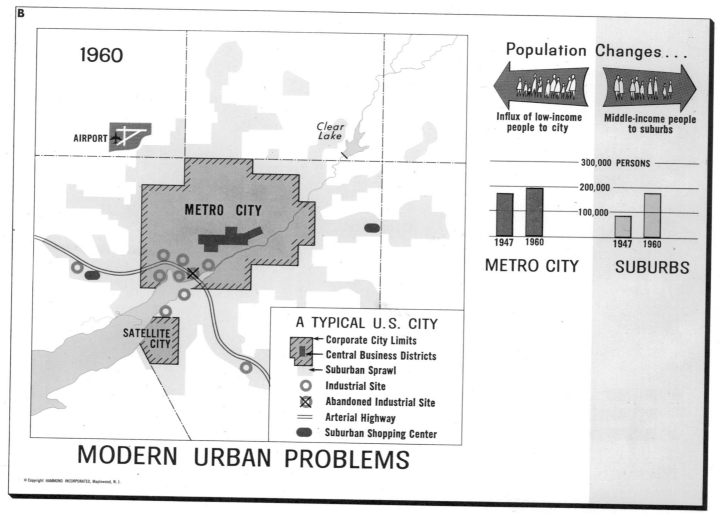

U-55

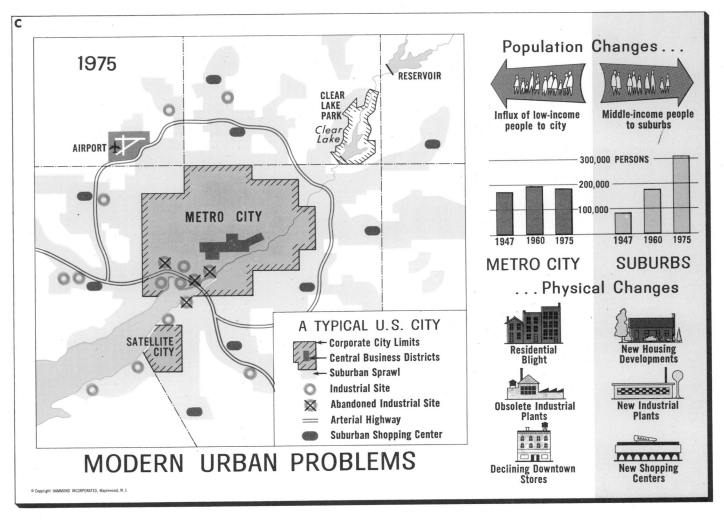

1975

RESERVOIR

CLEAR LAKE PARK

Clear Lake

AIRPORT

METRO CITY

SATELLITE CITY

A TYPICAL U.S. CITY

→ Corporate City Limits
■ Central Business Districts
→ Suburban Sprawl
◎ Industrial Site
✕ Abandoned Industrial Site
▭ Arterial Highway
⬮ Suburban Shopping Center

Population Changes...

Influx of low-income people to city

Middle-income people to suburbs

300,000 PERSONS
200,000
100,000

| 1947 | 1960 | 1975 | 1947 | 1960 | 1975 |

METRO CITY   SUBURBS

...Physical Changes

Residential Blight

New Housing Developments

Obsolete Industrial Plants

New Industrial Plants

Declining Downtown Stores

New Shopping Centers

MODERN URBAN PROBLEMS

© Copyright HAMMOND INCORPORATED, Maplewood, N. J.

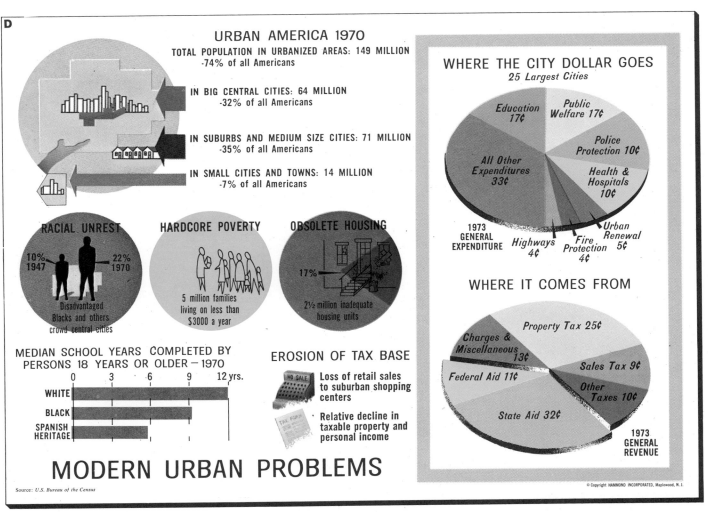

URBAN AMERICA 1970

TOTAL POPULATION IN URBANIZED AREAS: 149 MILLION
-74% of all Americans

IN BIG CENTRAL CITIES: 64 MILLION
-32% of all Americans

IN SUBURBS AND MEDIUM SIZE CITIES: 71 MILLION
-35% of all Americans

IN SMALL CITIES AND TOWNS: 14 MILLION
-7% of all Americans

RACIAL UNREST

10% 1947   22% 1970

Disadvantaged Blacks and others crowd central cities

HARDCORE POVERTY

5 million families living on less than $3000 a year

OBSOLETE HOUSING

17%

2½ million inadequate housing units

MEDIAN SCHOOL YEARS COMPLETED BY PERSONS 18 YEARS OR OLDER — 1970

0   3   6   9   12 yrs.

WHITE
BLACK
SPANISH HERITAGE

EROSION OF TAX BASE

NO SALE — Loss of retail sales to suburban shopping centers

TAX FORM — Relative decline in taxable property and personal income

WHERE THE CITY DOLLAR GOES
25 Largest Cities

Education 17¢
Public Welfare 17¢
Police Protection 10¢
Health & Hospitals 10¢
Urban Renewal 5¢
Fire Protection 4¢
Highways 4¢
All Other Expenditures 33¢

1973 GENERAL EXPENDITURE

WHERE IT COMES FROM

Property Tax 25¢
Sales Tax 9¢
Other Taxes 10¢
State Aid 32¢
Federal Aid 11¢
Charges & Miscellaneous 13¢

1973 GENERAL REVENUE

MODERN URBAN PROBLEMS

Source: *U.S. Bureau of the Census*

© Copyright HAMMOND INCORPORATED, Maplewood, N. J.

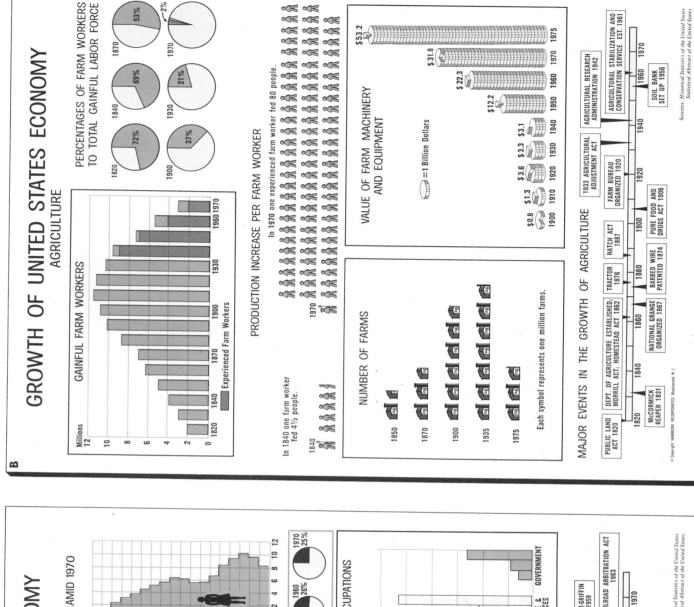

GROWTH OF UNITED STATES ECONOMY
AGRICULTURE

PERCENTAGES OF FARM WORKERS TO TOTAL GAINFUL LABOR FORCE

GROWTH OF UNITED STATES ECONOMY

GAINFUL FARM WORKERS

PRODUCTION INCREASE PER FARM WORKER

In 1840 one farm worker fed 4½ people.

In 1970 one experienced farm worker fed 80 people.

VALUE OF FARM MACHINERY AND EQUIPMENT

= 1 Billion Dollars

NUMBER OF FARMS

Each symbol represents one million farms.

MAJOR EVENTS IN THE GROWTH OF AGRICULTURE

Sources: Historical Statistics of the United States; Statistical Abstract of the United States

© Copyright HAMMOND INCORPORATED, Maplewood, N.J.

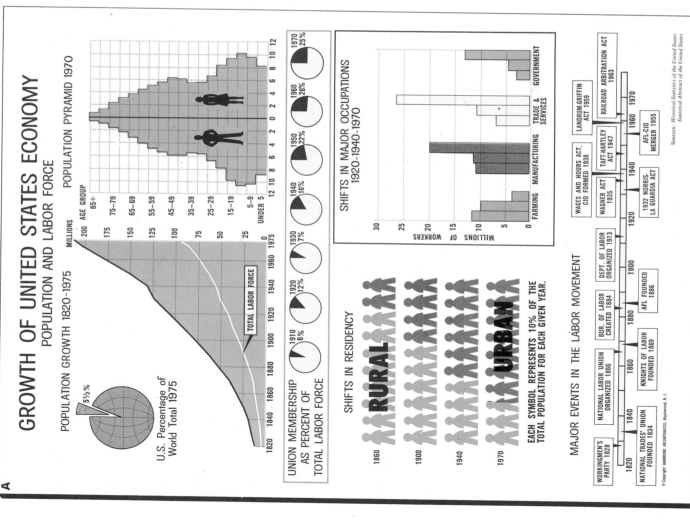

GROWTH OF UNITED STATES ECONOMY
POPULATION AND LABOR FORCE

POPULATION GROWTH 1820-1975

POPULATION PYRAMID 1970

U.S. Percentage of World Total 1975

UNION MEMBERSHIP AS PERCENT OF TOTAL LABOR FORCE

SHIFTS IN RESIDENCY

RURAL

URBAN

EACH SYMBOL REPRESENTS 10% OF THE TOTAL POPULATION FOR EACH GIVEN YEAR.

SHIFTS IN MAJOR OCCUPATIONS 1920-1940-1970

MAJOR EVENTS IN THE LABOR MOVEMENT

Sources: Historical Statistics of the United States; Statistical Abstract of the United States

© Copyright HAMMOND INCORPORATED, Maplewood, N.J.

GROWTH OF UNITED STATES ECONOMY
NATIONAL PRODUCT AND INCOME

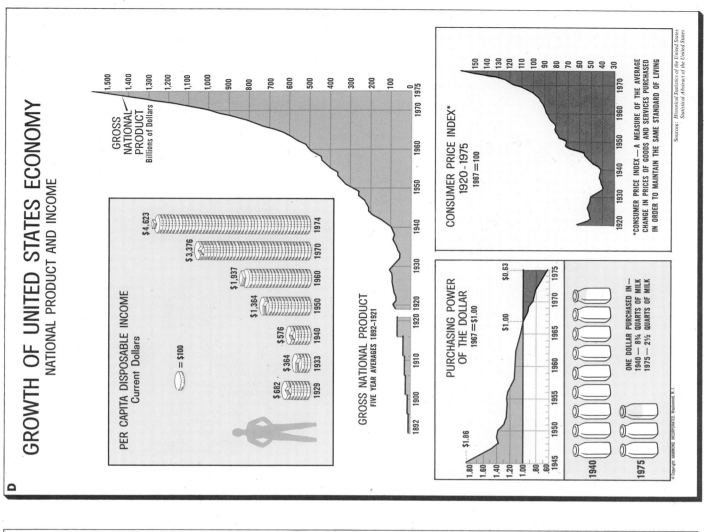

GROSS NATIONAL PRODUCT
Billions of Dollars

PER CAPITA DISPOSABLE INCOME
Current Dollars

= $100

$682 — 1929
$364 — 1933
$576 — 1940
$1,364 — 1950
$1,937 — 1960
$3,376 — 1970
$4,623 — 1974

GROSS NATIONAL PRODUCT
FIVE YEAR AVERAGES 1892-1921

CONSUMER PRICE INDEX*
1920 - 1975
1967 = 100

*CONSUMER PRICE INDEX — A MEASURE OF THE AVERAGE CHANGE IN PRICES OF GOODS AND SERVICES PURCHASED IN ORDER TO MAINTAIN THE SAME STANDARD OF LIVING

PURCHASING POWER OF THE DOLLAR
1967 = 1.00

$1.86
$1.00
$0.63

ONE DOLLAR PURCHASED IN —
1940 — 8¾ QUARTS OF MILK
1975 — 2½ QUARTS OF MILK

1940
1975

Sources: Historical Statistics of the United States
Statistical Abstract of the United States

© Copyright HAMMOND INCORPORATED, Maplewood, N.J.

D

GROWTH OF UNITED STATES ECONOMY
TRANSPORTATION

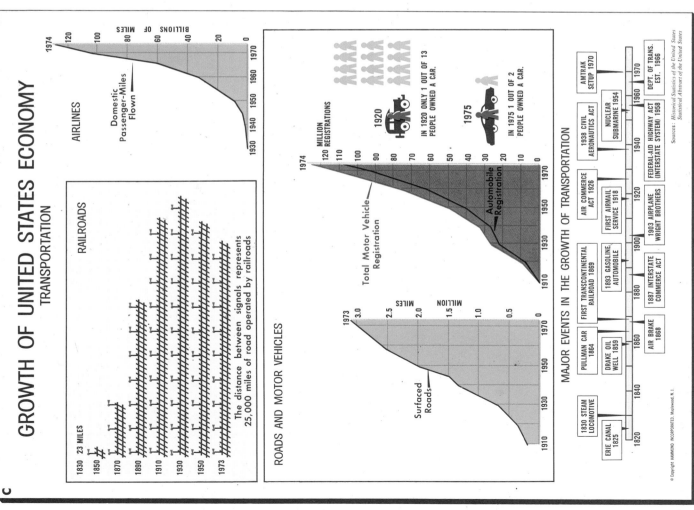

AIRLINES
Domestic Passenger-Miles Flown

BILLIONS OF MILES

1974 — 120

RAILROADS

1830 23 MILES
1850
1870
1890
1910
1930
1950
1973

MILES

The distance between signals represents 25,000 miles of road operated by railroads

ROADS AND MOTOR VEHICLES

MILLION REGISTRATIONS

1974 — 120

Total Motor Vehicle Registration

Automobile Registration

1920
IN 1920 ONLY 1 OUT OF 13 PEOPLE OWNED A CAR.

1975
IN 1975 1 OUT OF 2 PEOPLE OWNED A CAR.

MILES   MILLION

1973 — 3.0

Surfaced Roads

MAJOR EVENTS IN THE GROWTH OF TRANSPORTATION

ERIE CANAL 1825
1830 STEAM LOCOMOTIVE
DRAKE OIL WELL 1859
AIR BRAKE 1868
PULLMAN CAR 1864
FIRST TRANSCONTINENTAL RAILROAD 1869
1887 INTERSTATE COMMERCE ACT
1893 GASOLINE AUTOMOBILE
1903 AIRPLANE WRIGHT BROTHERS
FIRST AIRMAIL SERVICE 1918
AIR COMMERCE ACT 1926
1938 CIVIL AERONAUTICS ACT
FEDERAL-AID HIGHWAY ACT (INTERSTATE SYSTEM) 1958
NUCLEAR SUBMARINE 1954
AMTRAK SETUP 1970
DEPT. OF TRANS. EST. 1966

Sources: Historical Statistics of the United States
Statistical Abstract of the United States

© Copyright HAMMOND INCORPORATED, Maplewood, N.J.

C

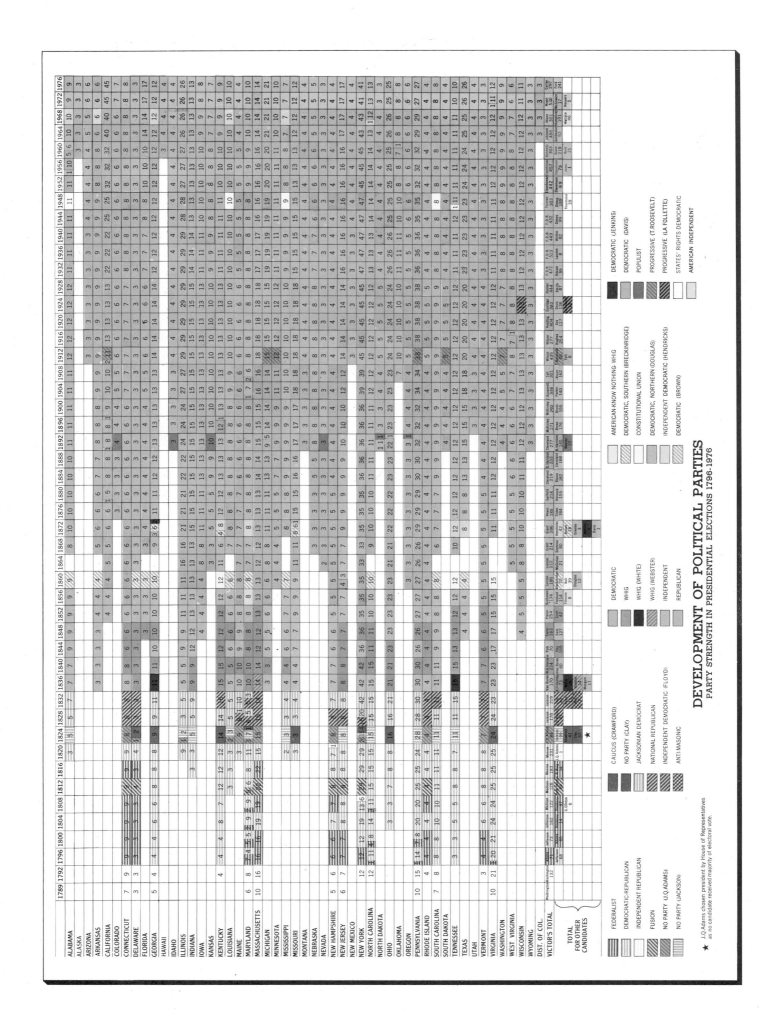

DEVELOPMENT OF POLITICAL PARTIES
PARTY STRENGTH IN PRESIDENTIAL ELECTIONS 1796-1976

★ J.Q.Adams chosen president by House of Representatives as no candidate received majority of electoral vote.

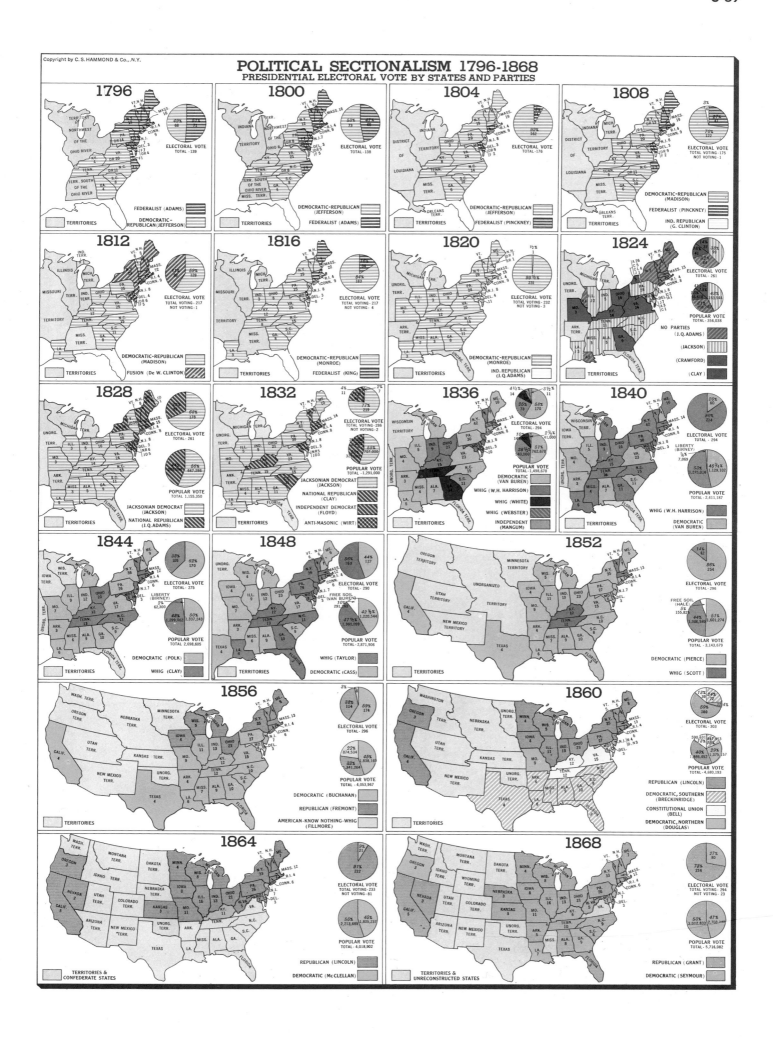

POLITICAL SECTIONALISM 1796-1868
PRESIDENTIAL ELECTORAL VOTE BY STATES AND PARTIES

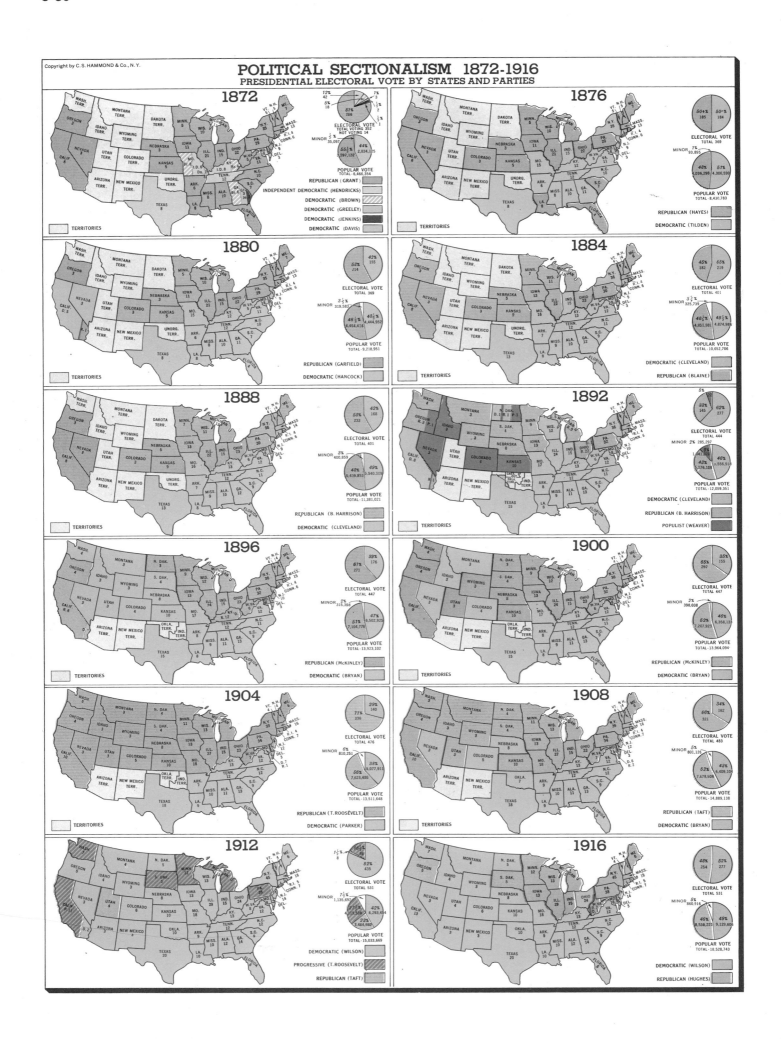

POLITICAL SECTIONALISM 1872-1916
PRESIDENTIAL ELECTORAL VOTE BY STATES AND PARTIES

Copyright by C.S. HAMMOND & Co., N.Y.

POLITICAL SECTIONALISM 1920-1964
PRESIDENTIAL ELECTORAL VOTE BY STATES AND PARTIES

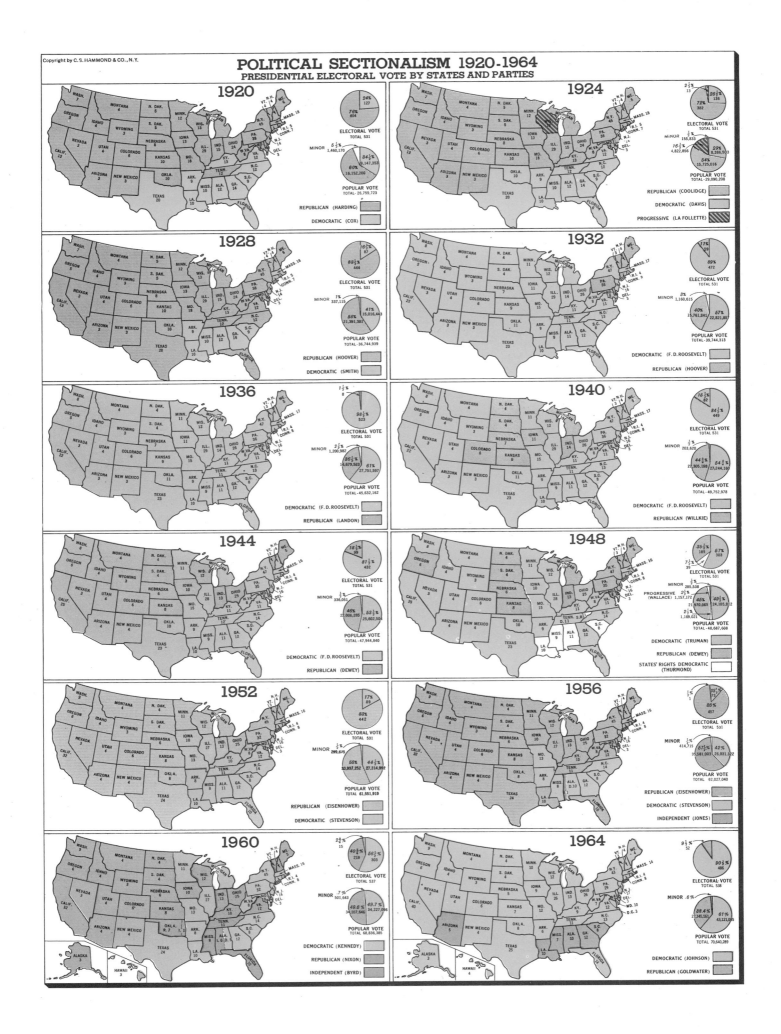

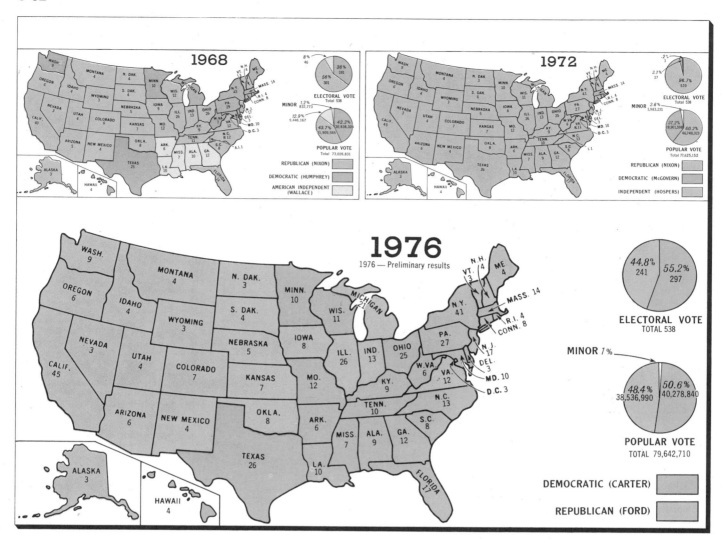

PRESIDENTS OF THE UNITED STATES

No.	Name	Politics	Native State	Age at Inauguration	Age at Death	No.	Name	Politics	Native State	Age at Inauguration	Age at Death
1	George Washington	Federalist	Va.	57	67	21	Chester Alan Arthur	Republican	Vt.	50	56
2	John Adams	Federalist	Mass.	61	90	22	Grover Cleveland	Democrat	N.J.	47	71
3	Thomas Jefferson	Rep.-Dem.	Va.	57	83	23	Benjamin Harrison	Republican	Ohio	55	67
4	James Madison	Rep.-Dem.	Va.	57	85	24	Grover Cleveland	Democrat	N.J.	55	71
5	James Monroe	Rep.-Dem.	Va.	58	73	25	William McKinley	Republican	Ohio	54	58
6	John Quincy Adams	Rep.-Dem.	Mass.	57	80	26	Theodore Roosevelt	Republican	N.Y.	42	60
7	Andrew Jackson	Democrat	S.C.	61	78	27	William Howard Taft	Republican	Ohio	51	72
8	Martin Van Buren	Democrat	N.Y.	54	79	28	Woodrow Wilson	Democrat	Va.	56	67
9	William Henry Harrison	Whig	Va.	68	68	29	Warren G. Harding	Republican	Ohio	55	57
10	John Tyler	Whig	Va.	51	71	30	Calvin Coolidge	Republican	Vt.	51	60
11	James Knox Polk	Democrat	N.C.	49	53	31	Herbert Clark Hoover	Republican	Iowa	54	90
12	Zachary Taylor	Whig	Va.	64	65	32	Franklin D. Roosevelt	Democrat	N.Y.	51	63
13	Millard Fillmore	Whig	N.Y.	50	74	33	Harry S. Truman	Democrat	Mo.	60	88
14	Franklin Pierce	Democrat	N.H.	48	64	34	Dwight D. Eisenhower	Republican	Texas	62	78
15	James Buchanan	Democrat	Pa.	65	77	35	John F. Kennedy	Democrat	Mass.	43	46
16	Abraham Lincoln	Republican	Ky.	52	56	36	Lyndon B. Johnson	Democrat	Texas	55	64
17	Andrew Johnson	Democrat	N.C.	56	66	37	Richard M. Nixon	Republican	Calif.	56	....
18	Ulysses Simpson Grant	Republican	Ohio	46	63	38	Gerald R. Ford	Republican	Mich.	61	....
19	Rutherford B. Hayes	Republican	Ohio	54	70	39	James E. Carter, Jr.	Democrat	Ga.	52	....
20	James Abram Garfield	Republican	Ohio	49	49						

Index

This index lists historically important places, areas, events and geographical features appearing on the maps of the United States History Atlas. Each entry is followed by the page number on which the name appears. The letters following the page number designate a particular map on pages containing more than one map. Names that appear on more than one map are indexed to the map or maps portraying the place at its most historically significant period.

For
Alan and Galip

First American Edition 2019
Kane Miller, A Division of EDC Publishing

Text copyright © Kate and Jol Temple, 2018
Illustrations copyright © Terri Rose Bayton, 2018

First published by Scholastic Press, a division of Scholastic Australia Pty
Limited in 2018. This edition published under license from Scholastic
Australia Pty Limited.

For information contact:
Kane Miller, A Division of EDC Publishing
PO Box 470663
Tulsa, OK 74147-0663
www.kanemiller.com
www.usbornebooksandmore.com
www.edcpub.com

Library of Congress Control Number: 2018958206
Printed in China
1 2 3 4 5 6 7 8 9 10
ISBN: 978-1-61067-902-2

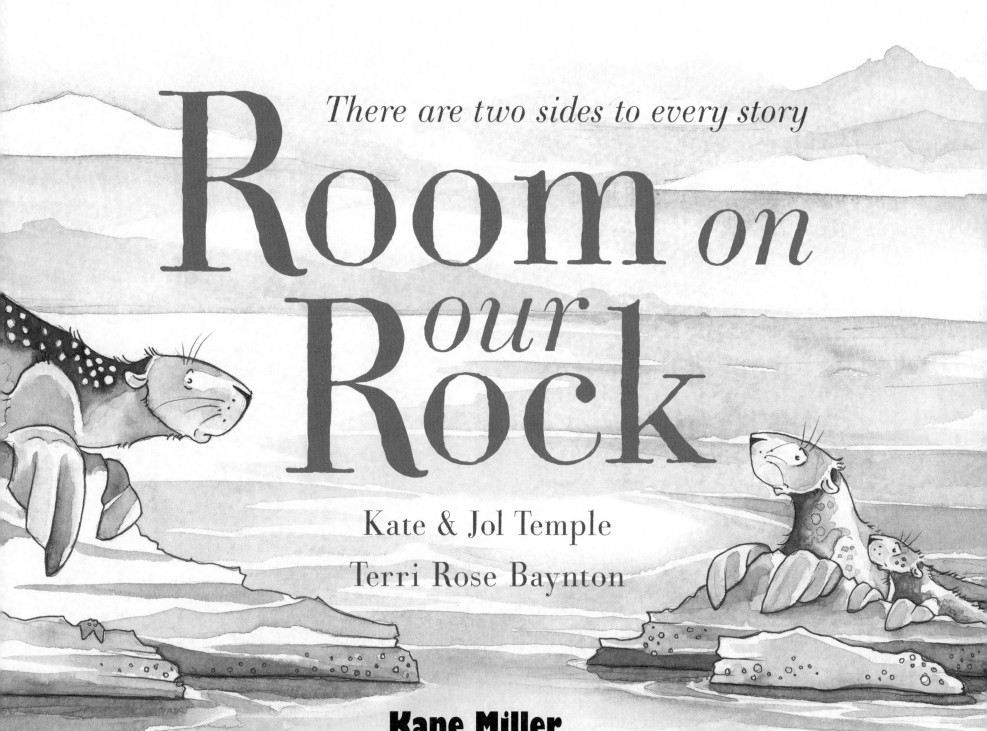

There are two sides to every story

Room on our Rock

Kate & Jol Temple

Terri Rose Baynton

Kane Miller

A DIVISION OF EDC PUBLISHING

There's *no room* on our rock

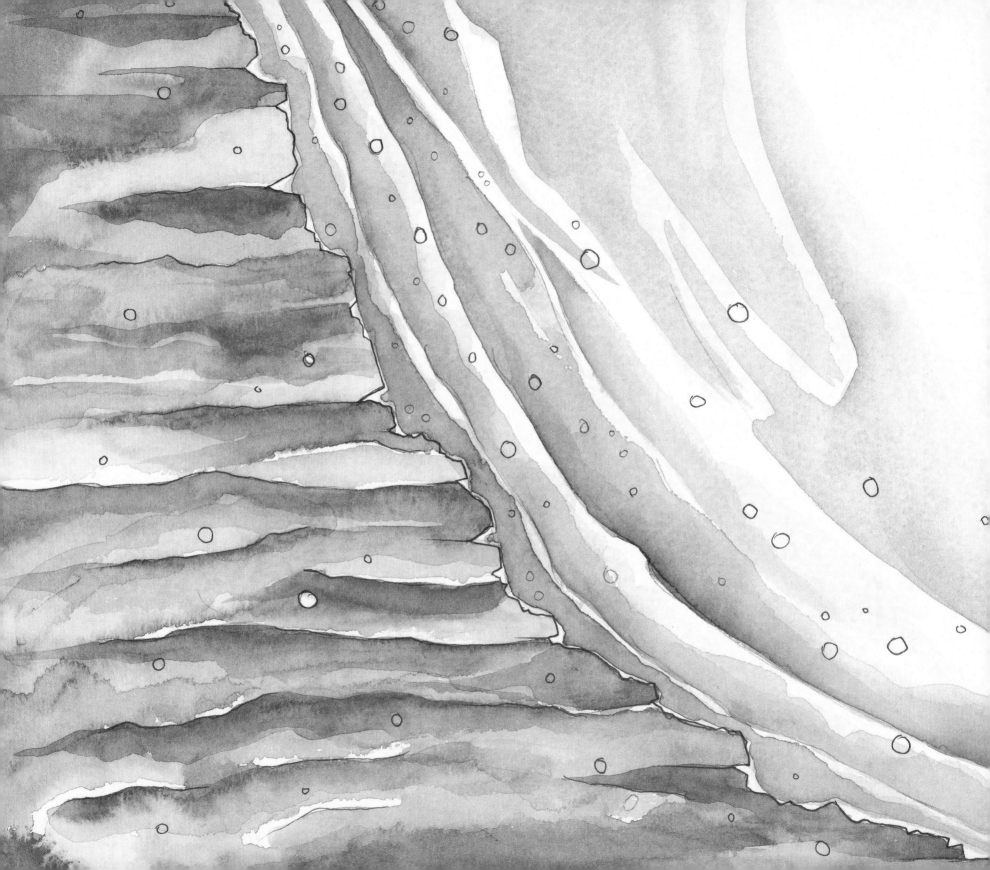

So it's
ridiculous to say

There's space for *plenty more*

You'll *never* hear us say

You're *welcome* here

This rock is *ours*

Go back to

your own

You know *you can't*

Make our rock your *home*

This *is no* place to be

You have to *leave* right now

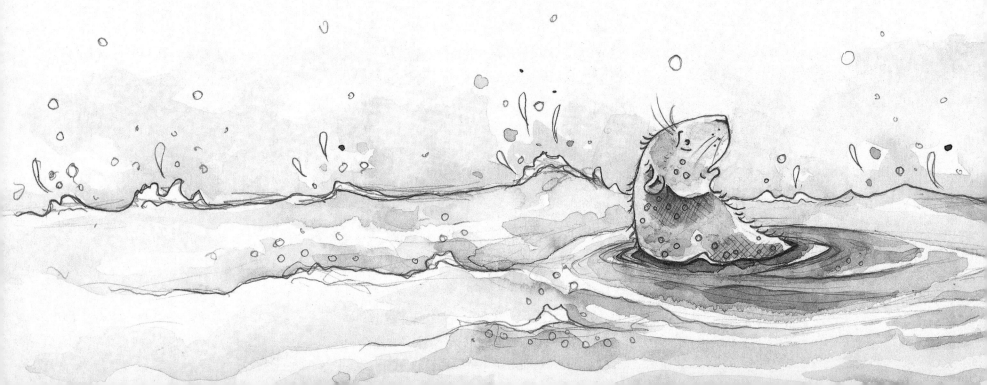

As you can
plainly see

Now turn around.

No room on this rock? Can it be true?

Read *back* to *front* for another point of view.